HEMMA LOMAX & ASHLEY DUBRIWNY

The Art of Ideation

For Culture Building

Copyright © 2024 by Hemma Lomax & Ashley Dubriwny

All rights reserved. No part of this publication may be reproduced, stored or transmitted in any form or by any means, electronic, mechanical, photocopying, recording, scanning, or otherwise without written permission from the publisher. It is illegal to copy this book, post it to a website, or distribute it by any other means without permission.

Hemma Lomax & Ashley Dubriwny asserts the moral right to be identified as the author of this work.

Hemma Lomax & Ashley Dubriwny has no responsibility for the persistence or accuracy of URLs for external or third-party Internet Websites referred to in this publication and does not guarantee that any content on such Websites is, or will remain, accurate or appropriate.

Designations used by companies to distinguish their products are often claimed as trademarks. All brand names and product names used in this book and on its cover are trade names, service marks, trademarks and registered trademarks of their respective owners. The publishers and the book are not associated with any product or vendor mentioned in this book. None of the companies referenced within the book have endorsed the book.

First edition

This book was professionally typeset on Reedsy.
Find out more at reedsy.com

This book is dedicated to our families and friends, for being a constant source of joy, hope, ideas, and inspiration.

It is also a tribute to all of you kind culture builders, who continue to do hard things well. Together, you make the world a better place to work, live, and play.

"All ideas grow out of other ideas."

Anish Kapoor

Contents

Introduction	1
1 Bright Ideas for Engagement	6
2 Bright Ideas for Training	27
3 Bright Ideas for Codes of Conduct	43
4 Bright Ideas for Influencing Leaders	55
5 Bright Ideas for Artificial Intelligence	66
6 Bright Ideas for Investigations	80
7 Bright Ideas for Crowdsourcing Intelligence	92
8 A Guide to Peer Ideation	108
Conclusion	121
Join the Community	122
Also by Hemma Lomax & Ashley Dubriwny	124

Introduction

A guide for culture builders designed to encourage peer ideation, the crowdsourcing of intelligence, and the sharing of best practices.

Ashley

It was a calm, sunny day in Chicago, but inside, my nerves were a tempest storming about in my rib cage. It was the *Society of Corporate Compliance and Ethics's 22nd Compliance & Ethics Institute* and I wasn't sure how my group's presentation on story building would go over with the crowd later that day.

My colleagues and I found our way to an empty table that soon filled with an eclectic group of ethics and compliance professionals taking advantage of the lunch buffet before afternoon sessions.

We had government folks, corporate powerhouses, non-profits, and a fair representation of large and small organizations. From designer blazers to logo-branded hoodies, our lunch table was a veritable sampling of individuals leading the charge for a culture of integrity.

Somewhere between bites, the polite small talk became an energized exchange of ideas. From baking brownies to designing custom cartoons, we laughed over our shared challenges and out-of-the-box solutions.

Soon, I realized I was no longer vibrating with anxiety over the coming presentation because I was immersed in a world of engaging, relatable stories.

At one point, a woman across the table from me rummaged through her canvas conference bag, pushing aside the remnants of her lunch to make room for a giant notebook. Scribbling away at the table, she smiled and whispered, "I come here for the ideas!"

At that moment, the vibrant light of inspiration clicked on in my mind. Certainly, professionals come together for a myriad of reasons, but I believe that at the heart of our motivations, there is always the hope for what's new, the ideas we can take away to keep our work, our organizations, and our minds reaching for what's next. Who doesn't want to be leading the race toward effectiveness or at least keeping up with the pacesetters?

So, if we're all here to gather ideas and build from one another's stories in the session rooms, at the lunch tables, and refilling our cups at that mercifully well-stocked tea and coffee station, why not create the space to ideate with intentionality?

Hemma

I arrived at the room on time, knowing that this story-building session would likely be over-subscribed, and I found that the only spare seats were at the front of the room. Undeterred, I grabbed my spot and settled in next to my friend Sarah, the sponsor of our *Great Women in Compliance Podcast*.

Ashley opened the session with an enchanting story. She transported

INTRODUCTION

us to a dawn visit to the fields at the Nature Conservancy's Tall Grass Prairie Preserve in Osage County, Oklahoma, where 30 years prior, 300 buffalo had been reintroduced after a 150-year absence. She had arrived in the earliest crisp morning hours in boots that weren't warm enough, with the pain of frozen fingers wrapped around a cup of hot chocolate, just in time to feel the ground below her trembling as that very herd of buffalo charged as part of a stampede, puffs of cold air visible on their breath, and with the glorious morning-sunrise burning at their backs.

With this simple story, Ashley invited us to experience the reverberations of the magnificent buffalo stampede and witness the brilliant orange sunrise over the frozen Oklahoma plains. She awakened all our senses and connected us to the specific moment as if we were there with her. She showed us the power of story and then shared a story-building method for all of us to leverage in our own work. I was captivated and turned to Sarah with wide eyes of excitement. I could tell she felt the same way, and we immediately agreed that we must invite Ashley and her co-presenters to be guests on the podcast.

At the end of the session, we took advantage of our front-seat positions to approach Ashley and thank her for her presentation. We immediately started discussing ways to leverage her story-building skills to benefit the wider compliance community. We agreed that inspiration for stories is everywhere. The ideas flowed, and plans were made to continue to scale the creativity together. We soon recorded a Great Women in Compliance podcast episode together on the 'Art and Science of Story Building,' but that was just the next stop on our adventure together, and we were hungry for more - excited about the next right thing.

Once we began the ideation process together, we realized we had many more quests ahead. We asked ourselves, how do we bring the idea that inspiration is everywhere to our wider community? How do we tap on the shoulder of the story builder in all of us? We knew we needed a space for all those friends who, like us, COME FOR THE IDEAS! Together, we could be creators of the culture, not just consumers. Our combined innovation meant we weren't limited to our own ideas.

What if we could replicate the magic of the annual conferences with something more sustainable to call upon when we needed it? Could we form an 'ideation station' that we could visit at any time, knowing that the 'inspiration express' would come through with new ideas and a vision for ongoing collaboration? We knew that this work was much bigger than a conference session. The connection, the sharing, the peer support, and the endless combinations of innovation could grow beyond one hour to create a peer ideation space for these culture builders beyond the session room, and beyond our own experiences.

This is how the idea for this book and the companion LinkedIn group came about as Ashley and I continued to bounce ideas at each other and iterate and grow. We hope you will enjoy some of the brightest and best ideas we have collected in this book for an array of culture-building challenges and opportunities. Join the *Ideation Station* LinkedIn Group using the QR code below to find more content, connect with other members, and share your favorite ideas.

While you might come for the ideas, we also want to leave you with the skill of peer ideation. We don't mind throwing you our finest fish, but we would rather remind everyone how to fish so we can do hard things well and move towards the fine art of sushi-making together. The magic of crowdsourcing ideas can be replicated in your organizations

INTRODUCTION

and networks using a versatile peer coaching method, allowing you to continue to ideate with peer support and have an outsized impact.

This book is for the ideators and story builders in each of you.

1

Bright Ideas for Engagement

A Note from Hemma

I landed in São Paolo a day early, filled with anticipation but also exhausted, wanting to recover from the long flight before launching into a full week of presentations and meetings. I had always wanted to visit Brazil to experience the sights and sounds of Carnival. Still, I never thought my first trip would be meeting with over 200 sales executives to discuss corporate ethics and compliance. But for now, my focus was navigating the sprawling airport and finding Marcel, the driver who had arranged to meet me.

It turns out Marcel had collected many illustrious guests from this airport, and soon I realized I was sitting in the same seat as cultural royalty as he shared with me the tours he had led with a famous photographer, several US rap artists, and one member of a legendary rock band. Rather than spend the weekend in my hotel room, preparing for my meetings, it occurred to me that I should follow in these famous footsteps and seize the chance to see São Paolo with Marcel.

Jet lag be damned, I decided on spontaneity, and we settled on a time to start my tour the next day. With just a bottle of water and an iPhone, I set out on a whistle-stop tour of the beautiful Ibirapuera park, the winding floors of the Fundação Bienal museum, the vibrant Beco de Batman (Batman Alley) with jaw-droppingly fabulous murals rich with intense color and stories, and a sprawling local rooftop bar to try some delicious food where I saw the entire city from a bird's eye view, all before heading to meet some colleagues for a late dinner at the local Figueira Rubaiyat restaurant, an incredible structure which wrapped around a magnificent 200-year-old fig tree.

Many photos were taken as I inhaled this veritable feast for the eyes. As I returned late to my hotel room, I was in equal parts delighted with my impulse to go on a guided city tour and anxious about not spending the weekend preparing for my presentation for the Brazil team all-hands meeting the next day.

While thinking about what I wanted to say and absentmindedly scrolling through the photographs I had taken, it hit me. If my goal is to build trust and persuade my colleagues in São Paolo that we don't want to be just a US-centric company, I could do more than translate a couple of slides into Portuguese. I could center the presentation around the beautiful images I had captured of their city that day. Suddenly, inspiration struck as I leveraged the picture of the Trojan horse from the Bienal to explain that I wasn't here to look for wrongdoing. I showed the image of the 200-year-old banyan tree stretching out of the windows of the Figueira Rubaiyat restaurant as a metaphor for how foundational and pervasive a culture of integrity could be. I asked the teams to help me stretch beyond the region and model that culture globally.

It turned out that inspiration was everywhere once I knew the messages I wanted to convey and kept the specific audience in mind. I wanted them to know we cared about them and their well-being and wanted their perspectives and engagement to ensure we were serving their needs and modeling global consciousness as a company. You can imagine this presentation's powerful and immediate impact on establishing trust. The images spoke a thousand words and set the scene as I met my colleagues in Brazil for the first time.

The Banyan Tree, located inside the Figueira Rubaiyat Restaurant, was planted in the 1890s in the Jardins district, long before it was a thriving gastronomic center.

Vibrant murals in Beco de Batman (Batman Alley), in the Vila Madalena neighborhood of São Paolo, Brazil. Artist Unknown.

More stunning murals in Beco de Batman (Batman Alley). Artist Unknown.

An image of the Trojan Horse as part of artist Kidlat Tahmik's installation Killing Us Softly .... with their SPAMS ... (Songs, Prayers, Alphabets, Myths, Superheros ...) (2023) at the 35th Bienal de São Paolo.

Our Concept for Engagement Ideation

Know your audience

Every speaker understands that the first rule of speaking is to know the audience. Challenge your ideas about what that means. As the story above illustrates, this can mean demonstrating that you care about getting to know your audience and what matters to them. Beyond moving away from unwieldy acronyms or legal speak, consider the barriers between your team and those you serve across functions and geographies.

Whether you work in health care, technology, finance, or non-profit, all teams are made up of individuals who care deeply about the product, service, or necessary good they believe they are doing in the world. Equally, they experience pain points, frustrations, and inequities. Take the time to know your industry, your organization, and the individuals doing the work. You might be surprised at how effective you become at engaging individuals and teams when you discover and show concern for the things that matter most to them.

If you support a global organization, consider that staff outside the country where the organization is headquartered can sometimes feel disconnected and undervalued by the larger organization. Imagine attempting to engage with a Code of Conduct or policies that are poorly translated or only available in the language spoken at headquarters. These materials, meant to provide foundational guidance, are rendered useless or at least damaging to trust. It's not uncommon for translations to be left off the project plan, underfunded, or an afterthought.

Building a globally inclusive culture means aspiring to engage everyone. A pivotal component of this engagement is to make a concerted effort to secure translation services, prioritize the most important communications and resources for the global teams for translation, and then vet the translations to ensure they are authentic and accurate for those who will rely on them.

You don't have to stop at translating key policy documents and training. When you create entertaining posts on the organization's social feed, awareness-building cartoons, quick guides, or casual updates, consider doing so in your organization's most used languages and not only in the primary language.

Want to build considerable global culture capital and practice global consciousness? Deliver some of your key communications in the organization's second or third most used language with the primary language offered in subtitles. While these efforts are only the beginning of fostering a global focus, they are meaningful to teams and individuals outside the city or country where the organization is headquartered and can open the door for authentic global engagement.

Embed your work

A candid communications leader once read her compliance team's list of announcement requests and, with a dry smile, remarked, "You know your team isn't the *only* one with a message for staff at this organization, right?"

She wasn't wrong. Is there any end to the corporate communications sent to any one employee? Who hasn't felt overwhelmed by a barrage of messages, notices, Slack or other direct messaging alerts, courtesy emails, and monthly newsletters?

Radical empathy and compassion will drive culture builders to examine what they can do to improve this modern-day phenomenon for partners and stakeholders. You might start by identifying your organization's most popular communication channels, knowing it may vary by function. If everyone enjoys the CEO's quarterly quip or HR's monthly take on what's hot, consider embedding your message within those popular mediums. If the sales team already has rules of engagement, pepper those with the most relevant compliance messages rather than setting out a separate set of rules.

It may take some convincing to grab real estate in the communication channels of other functions, but it will positively promote the perception of the person or group who agrees to highlight your message, create less work for you, and offer your audience one less email, blog, or newsletter to review.

The same idea applies to meetings, learning, surveys, assessments, and Board presentations. Be pervasive to be persuasive. The economies of scale from combined efforts are enormous. At the next board or audit committee meeting, could each function talk about how they have mitigated relevant risk without the compliance team having to do a separate round-up? Could you add some questions to an existing company-wide survey rather than having a separate culture survey or risk assessment?

On the receiving end, people will feel seen and heard if we meet them where they are rather than making them come to us for our messages and go elsewhere to engage with another function. Empathy and understanding of the user experience and sentiment are essential, and a lack of the same will be a barrier to communication. To steal an idea from customer service, improve your customer satisfaction (C-SAT) and net promoter scores (NPS) by building a culture of engagement around the user perspective and experience.

You might partner with an internal communications team to identify a holistic communication strategy within your organization. Learn together who owns the most-read newsletters, how frequently they are published, and what functions or groups receive them. Use that information to determine where to publish key messages throughout the year and strategize for maximum impact with minimum disruption.

Streamline your message

Have you ever had a brilliant idea that got whisked away and plopped onto the proverbial conveyor belt in the factory for review and approval by all? On the other side of the red-line nightmare, you are left with a distorted or diluted version of your message that is no longer concise and accessible. With everyone's additions, edits, and amendments, you now have a Frankenstein of a project and the key message cannot be discerned because it's been buried under a mountain of good intentions.

Believe it or not, when you include "everything but the kitchen sink" in your work, you put your effectiveness down on the altar of "saving your assets." If you have an important message, make it as brief as possible. One of our favorite refrains is to be brief, be relevant, and be gone. This works equally for wedding speeches, board presentations, and employee communications. Highlight what is most important and drive home that message in the most simplistic way possible.

BJ Fogg, author of *Tiny Habits* and developer of the *Fogg Behavior Model*, says that the likelihood of any behavior occurring (here, many employees engaging with your content) depends on motivation, ability, and prompts. Even if the stars have aligned so that someone wants to read your communication and you have successfully prompted them to do so at an opportune time, you will get in your own way if you make the actual message so cumbersome in length or language that they just aren't able to take it in. In this way, culture builders can learn a lot from how social media is designed, where user experience, ease of use, and timely nudges are paramount.

When planning learning and engagement, ask your training and communications teams, "Do we want a lot of useful information that a few people will read, or do we want a little key information that a lot of people will read?" Your answer might differ depending on the type of information and the team. However, it is important to consider the answer from the recipient's perspective and experience, not just the relative importance of the cause. If you're hoping to influence the entire organization to do expense reports differently or complete the annual compliance training, consider a message that is short, simple, and accessible.

Focus on your audience's journey

When you focus on your audience and map out their 'journey,' you can find innovative ways to reach them. In one case, a company lit up the skies with a drone show at the end of an event held by a competitor - a simple QR code on the drone allowed the competitor's customers to get free food at nearby food trucks. They also offered free ride-share rides to and from the competitor's venue. One agency placed billboard-style ads at a major metropolitan train station to share its values and mission with the populations it serves. Another company couldn't sponsor a significant event that their intended audience was attending, so instead, they put their message on the room keys of the local hotels where the audience was staying.

Inspired by these marketing geniuses, culture builders asked for access to an event app that was a mandatory download for the company's annual Sales Kick-Off event. This event was the one time in the year when the entire global sales team and leadership would convene in one city. On the first day of the event, a simple welcome to the city message came through the mobile app to all participants from the ethics and compliance team, with a courtesy link to the gifts and entertainment rules and forms.

An AI-generated image of a drone holding a QR code and a projection over a city onto the night sky. Scan the QR code to join our LinkedIn group for bonus content and community ideation.

Get current beyond your comfort

Whether we like it or not, the one constant in the world is change. Most of us no longer read a physical newspaper. Many lifelong morning news viewers find themselves scrolling social media for quick soundbites each day instead of tuning into a 30-minute broadcast. In our modern world, information is expertly curated to our interests, fast to process, and literally at our fingertips with strategic nudges to prompt us to engage repeatedly.

THE ART OF IDEATION

The preference for how information is consumed is evolving, and culture builders must keep pace. If your rule books or Codes of Conduct aren't mobile-friendly, you may have an entire generation less likely to view them. If you lean completely on memos, faxes, websites, emails, or instant messaging to convey relevant information, you may not be as effective as you'd like. We know that just like e-mail, the Internet and smartphones have disrupted how we consume information. At the time of writing, artificial intelligence (AI) has taken disruption to a new level.

Consider getting current just beyond your comfort zone. When you aren't afraid to live in this dynamic and unpredictable space, you'll find the limits of your ideation are ever-expanding. Don't be scared to experiment and think outside of the box. Take inspiration from the best marketing and engagement campaigns and see what you can replicate.

Combine ideas from other spaces and create something new to ignite your culture. This might include leveraging video shorts, podcasts, cartoons, comedy or improv, stickers, bookmarks, button pins, cookies, water bottle labels, balloons, QR codes, screensavers, virtual backgrounds, bot conversations, music, and, if the budget allows, even real drone shows to reach your audience, wherever they may be. Do you prefer low-cost/no-cost? A fun AI-generated image of a virtual drone show might do in lieu of the real thing.

Here's a Bright Idea

Map out the journey of your intended audience and meet them where they are. Are there teams you serve, who by virtue of their function, would not have access to company laptops? This will likely impact your communications strategy, including considering mobile-friendly content and funnels that don't require a computer. Some field teams lean heavily on mobile devices and outdoor signage with QR codes to direct them to the most current content and guidance. In some organizations, customer or product-facing field staff face a heightened risk for harassment, safety, and third-party issues, but they are also less likely to report problems.

In response, you can work with field leaders to provide signage with QR codes that link to your organization's Code of Conduct and Hotline so anyone at any time can have access to these resources. Clear and accessible pathways for speaking up could be made available to frontline or field staff. In the spirit of meeting your teams where they are, encourage your culture builders to get curious about how different teams prefer to communicate.

Perhaps your organization doesn't have staff operating in the field. However, you may have identified staff who need resources, support, and awareness but won't have opportunities to interact with the primary business communication and training channels. Getting curious about these teams and how they prefer to communicate will likely inspire solutions, but it requires ideating beyond the tried-and-true methods. The best way to find out what works for these teams is to ask them and create the solutions together.

As culture builders, we should regularly ask "what if" to ensure we think outside the boxes we may have created. This is a wonderful way to do a quick gap assessment and a superb method for brainstorming ideas to fill those gaps. For example, what if we could only collect three pieces of information as part of this upcoming survey - what would we ask? Or what if we asked the sales team for their ideas on what might be most helpful for them in a Code of Conduct - how might that change our approach to the annual refresh?

What if you could have a local team in your global organization drive your next communication strategy in a different language from that spoken at the head office? In one example, inspired by a children's play, culture builders considered using the phrase "Not my circus, not my monkeys" to drive engagement and discussion on the collective responsibility to speak up.

This idea encouraged team members to participate in creating a culture of active bystandership by drawing the lines for appropriate boundaries of tolerance. As it happens, this reference to monkeys and the circus is a Polish expression: Nie mój cyrk, nie moje małpy. On learning this, the culture builders seized the opportunity to request the help of the team members based in Poland to drive the campaign in Polish, with subtitles for the rest of the global workforce.

An image produced in Canva shows a cool monkey hovering within a circus tent with the Polish expression "Nie mój cyrk, nie moje małpy?" which translates into English as "Not my circus, not my monkey?"

What if you could use a catchy tune to help people remember your message? Modern memes need only reference a culturally iconic tune with 'updated' lyrics to captivate audiences in a memorable way. Anchoring your message to popular entertainment mediums is another way to gain the attention of your target audience and improve their recall of the message. Can you think of a popular song, proverb, maxim, advertisement, or holiday jingle that you could tweak and leverage to share a succinct but important message or behavioral nudge?

A meme developed in Canva with a fun play on the song 'Holding Out for a Hero' originally recorded by Bonnie Tyler (the artist pictured) as part of the Footloose movie soundtrack.

Our Challenge to You

Ask yourself:

- What are you selling as a function? Is it fear, safety, ease, peace of mind?
- What is your key message?
- How will you convey it?
- To whom?
- Who is the primary audience for this message?

- Will your usual or default approach be successful with this audience?
- Who else is interacting with your intended audience, and what opportunities are there to piggyback on those efforts?
- Is any translation needed, whether literal interpretation, images, or cultural references?

Consider:

- The most exciting and innovative marketing campaigns you have seen.
- How your team typically engages with your intended audience. (emails, office hours, intranet, investigations, annual training)
- The typical ways that your audience consumes information.
- Ways to make it effortless for your audience to come across your content.
- Mapping out your audience's journey and look for opportunities to pleasantly and helpfully surprise them along the way.
- Using the "what if" game with peers to critically analyze your plans, to think outside of the box, and to generate new ideas.

Parting Thoughts on Engagement

"The desire to reach the stars is ambitious. The desire to reach hearts is wise."
–Maya Angelou

Engagement is our highest form of currency when building culture and promoting behaviors that align with that culture. A healthy tone at the top means very little if it isn't communicated effectively and consistently to those we hope to impact, influence, and motivate.

If the advent of modern social media has taught us anything, it is that superb content is not enough. Culture builders need the right channels, the right timing and tone, the element of surprise and delight, and above all, the ease of experience to cultivate meaningful engagement.

Engagement for culture building is about winning hearts and minds. To do this, start with radical curiosity, empathy, and compassion for the audiences you are trying to reach. For that, inspiration is everywhere.

2

Bright Ideas for Training

A Note from Ashley

Have you ever tried to raise awareness about an important topic through training but found that your colleagues simply weren't engaged? I've stood on the precipice of utter failure with learning and engagement efforts and stumbled upon redemption in that dark, uncomfortable space.

It was one of those sudden spring days where gray skies give way to blue, and warm temperatures make you feel hopeful and childlike. It was also a Friday afternoon, and I had the simple task of delivering mandated training to a reluctant audience. No one was on time, no one made eye contact during introductions, and the leader of the team was huddled in a corner, noisily crunching away on a bag of extra crispy kettle chips. These folks had Friday afternoon energy. I knew the content was good, relevant, and important for this particular team, but at that moment, I wanted to give up and reschedule the training.

Instead, my co-facilitator and I continued, seemingly presenting only to one another. Then, about 15 minutes into the training, something magical changed everything. I shared a personal story. The story was simple and only took a few minutes to share. It added a touch of humanity to the material and brought the content to life, complete with the tragedy and triumph of a lived experience.

To my surprise, as the story unfolded, so did the team's engagement. Heads lifted around the room as gazes locked with my own. The room buzzed with attentive energy and I watched as shoulders leaned forward and heads nodded in understanding and empathy. When I paused at the end of the story, hands shot up across the room. Tentatively, then eagerly, attendees shared similar experiences, cloaked in the relief of being seen and heard, while others expressed surprise and compassion, as they were hearing these perspectives for the first time.

The story connected them to an experience that was familiar, shared, and important to that team. That connection gave deeper meaning to the training content and allowed those in the room to join in on a shared learning journey. I was surprised by the story's impact on our ability to connect with that Friday afternoon audience. Yet, the power of story has been wielded since the dawn of time to connect, teach, and influence.

Since that experience, I've prioritized storytelling in all the learnings and trainings I've developed. It's not uncommon for attendees of those learning experiences to express gratitude for the stories. Stories impact people and play a meaningful role in learning and connection. As culture builders, we, too, can wield the mighty power of story to engage, build awareness, and influence those we serve.

Our Concept for Training Ideation

Involve the learner

To substitute training for learning and communication for engagement, we must design for the user experience. This means being intentional and thoughtful about training designed to optimize engagement, interaction, application, and action. The word educate is based on the Latin word "educare" which means to "bring up, or rear" and is closely related to the Latin word "educere" which means to lead out, bring out, or draw out the lessons in a person, from a person, rather than simply providing those lessons. We like to think of this as creating a space where participants can be encouraged to think, discover, find answers, exchange thoughts and ideas, make informed decisions, and make the lessons their own.

Have a live audience? Make audience engagement a priority. Music can set the tone for the energy you hope to achieve as attendees join the room. This is also an excellent time to share stickers, button pins, pens, coasters, and other giveaway items that promote the hotline, the Code of Conduct, or the organization's values. Games, prizes, and celebrations will make the training exciting and go a long way in humanizing the facilitators to the audience. An approachable facilitator makes it easier for learners to speak up with questions and concerns and can improve the team's brand.

We know that many people shy away when asked to interact or engage in a training session. However, the challenge for culture builders is to find ways that work for a variety of learning styles. We don't want a race to the bottom where no one contributes; we want to find ways to ensure anyone can safely contribute, including anonymously, quietly, virtually, one-on-one, in small groups, in writing, in pictures, or from the back of the room. We can smartly design material meant to crowdsource and *educe* learning for the participants, not *reduce* it. To honor the collective brain power in the room is to leave no brain behind.

Take the learner on a journey

As indicated in the opening story of this chapter, you can't overestimate the power of storytelling to connect with learners. This is a way to take the learner on a journey and have participants feel involved in the learning experience. Shared stories bring the listener along, fully evoking the senses. Stories allow us to see ourselves in a character, one who ultimately represents our limited experience. In journeying with this character, we, too, can expand our thinking and knowledge and, thus, broaden our perspectives and potential for understanding.

The story experience increases engagement and retention of the message and creates an emotional connection with the content. Organizational psychologist Peg Neuhauser found that learning from a well-told story is remembered more accurately and far longer than learning from facts and figures. Similarly, psychologist Jerome Bruner's research suggests that facts are twenty times more likely to be remembered if they are part of a story.

Learning facts without context overloads our working memory, and we often lose those facts. However, learning through story adds context, which creates emotional resonance. This allows us to retain and even be influenced by the same facts that we might have otherwise forgotten.

Stories lend themselves to nearly all modalities of learning. Humans experience stories through reading books, articles, advertisements, and social media. We also experience stories through spoken word, music, and visual arts. As you, or your favorite AI buddy, explore stories for learning, open yourself to the multitude of pathways for sharing those stories. Consider mediums like podcasts, movie trailers, short form TikTok, Snapchat, or Triller videos, and more. You can draw from existing resources or employ tools like Articulate, Canva, or iMovie to design your own. Stories, in their innumerable forms of delivery, have the ultimate impact on your learner.

Make learning a quest or a challenge

Has anyone ever complained that your annual compliance training was too easy? This is a common refrain when training content is patronizingly basic, or multiple-choice testing questions have three absurdly incorrect answers alongside a blindingly obvious one. When the training isn't appropriately challenging, it will feel like a box-checking waste of time.

It is understandable that many professionals are on the fence about this concept, especially if you're deploying content to a wide range of learners. Keep your purpose in mind and allow it to be your ultimate guide as you develop your training. For most training designers, the purpose of a given training is to raise awareness around critical learnings that impact the integrity of the business. If this is your purpose, especially if you are designing for broad audiences, focus on the simplicity of your goal. This is not a time to challenge, trick, or confuse your learner. To build foundational awareness for a broad audience, develop training that is clear, organized, and accessible.

As you consider the purpose of your training be wary of a race to the bottom. Suppose your goal is to convey critical information that influences behavior. In that case, you might steer clear of distracting your learner from that primary purpose and use methods like summaries, examples, and jingles to reinforce memorization and absorption of the content.

If your goal is to teach the skills of analysis and decision-making, you will want opportunities to practice that skill with some nuance in your questions and answers. If you leverage a quiz to allow people to test out from taking the annual refresher training, you will want the quiz to help ensure the user has a basic grasp of the key concepts.

Who says learning can't be fun? In fact, research shows that when we are entertained during a learning experience, we improve our retention of the information conveyed during that experience. Lean into influencing your learners with fun by employing gamification for online learning or buzzers and prizes for in-person learning.

Tailor your training strategy for specific unmet needs

Before embarking on training development, take time to identify your objective and the key obstacles you might face in meeting that goal. Let's call those 'the root issues' and determine whether each of those is primarily a matter of Awareness, Skill, Culture, or Will. By strategically analyzing the training opportunities in this way, you will maximize the chance of meeting your objectives. This will save you time and ensure an effective, streamlined training plan.

Despite the temptation to set up training to influence all behaviors, Awareness and Skill gaps are the most likely to be addressed through traditional training methods. Culture and Will may be more challenging to tackle in the same way. A critical and often overlooked practice is accurately labeling objectives as issues of Skill, Awareness, Will, or Culture before launching the training plan.

What if you took a fresh look at your training objectives and used a simple analytical framework to ensure your training strategy is fit for purpose? Culture builders must first be clear on their objectives and understand the specific gaps they are trying to fill.

After identifying the goal and listing the root causes you want to tackle, you can ask yourself, is this an issue of Skill, Awareness, Will, or Culture (SAWC)? What is going on in relation to your goal at your organization? Are people unable, unaware, unwilling, unlikely, or some combination of the same? Labeling each issue in this way allows you to determine if training is likely to help solve the problem, might help, or would not help. Perhaps you need a different type of training or approach for each? This simple strategy allows teams to hone in on the key areas of focus that are most likely to be impacted by training.

Here's a Bright Idea, or Two

Designing your training strategy

Spice up your training strategy meeting and invite your culture builders to a SAWC (pronounced 'saucy') ideation exercise using the four-step model below.

Step One: Identify your specific culture objective. For this example, we have chosen the goal of creating a speak-up culture.

An image created in Canva showing a lady on a laptop

Step Two: Consider all of the possible reasons that your organization has not met that goal (whether at all or to your satisfaction). These root causes may be obstacles or existing conditions that have stood in the way of your specific goal. A survey, culture assessment, focus group, or even a simple chat with a few representative members of your organization can help with this step.

BRIGHT IDEAS FOR TRAINING

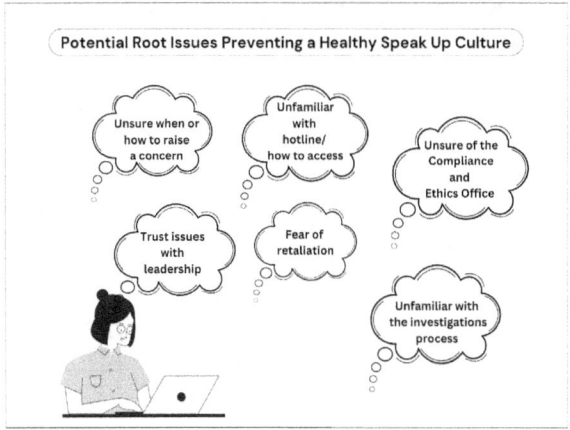

An image created in Canva showing thought bubbles with possible root issues.

Step Three: Create an Effective Training Map like the one below. Use it to assess each root issue and determine if each is primarily an issue of Skill, Awareness, Will, or Culture (or some combination). Are people in the current culture unable, unaware, unwilling, or unlikely?

THE ART OF IDEATION

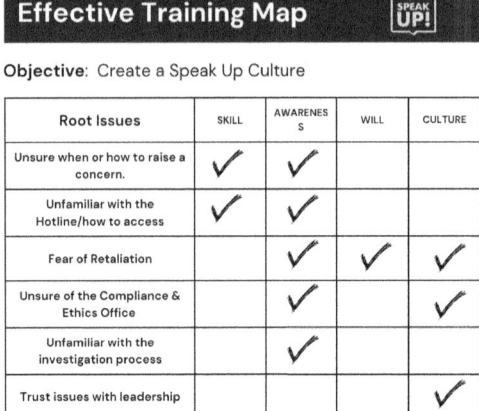

Training Map Created in Canva.

Step Four: Once you have identified whether a root issue is one of Skill, Awareness, Will, or Culture, you will be better prepared to design effective training to address that issue.

BRIGHT IDEAS FOR TRAINING

Effective Training Map SPEAK UP!

Objective: Create a Speak Up Culture

Root Issues	SKILL	AWARENESS	WILL	CULTURE	Is training an effective option for improving this issue?
Unsure when or how to raise a concern.	✓	✓			👍
Unfamiliar with the Hotline/how to access	✓	✓			👍
Fear of Retaliation		✓	✓	✓	?
Unsure of the Compliance & Ethics Office		✓		✓	?
Unfamiliar with the investigation process		✓			👍
Trust issues with leadership				✓	⊘

Training Map with training effectiveness scores, created in Canva.

Ideas for interactivity and inclusion

As a fair warning to your learners that your live training sessions will include some co-creative and interactive elements, you might share something like the slide below, complete with a personal Bitmoji, to indicate that through the co-creative sharing of intelligence and ideation, you can go beyond learning to fish, even learning to fish, and make beautiful artful "sushi" together.

Sample presentation slide created using Hemma's Bitmoji in Snapchat and based on the famous quote attributed to Benjamin Franklin, and Chinese Confucian philosopher Xun Kuang, replicated at the end of this chapter and

For virtual experiences, consider virtual polling tools like Mentimeter or PollEverywhere to create engagement opportunities for the virtual audience to participate, even anonymously. This allows participation without the need to raise hands or feel vulnerable in front of the group. As demonstrated in the sample below, you might offer multiple correct answers that participants can scale according to their comfort level. Who says you have to have wrong answers as an option?

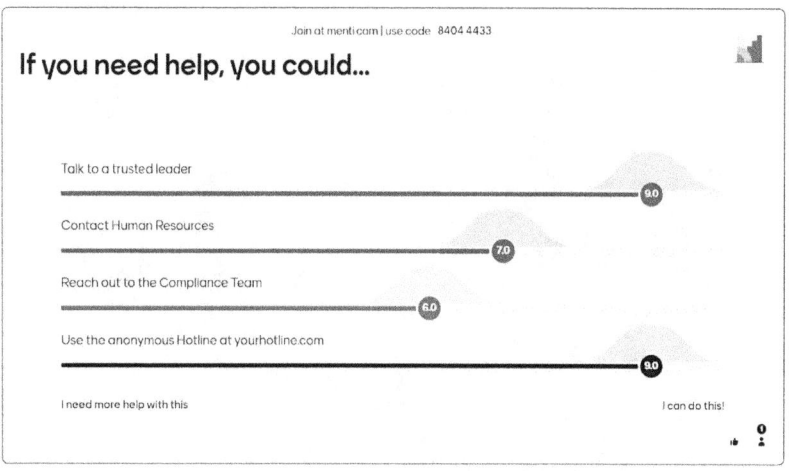

A sample poll created in Mentimeter allows participants to rate each response using four correct answers.

Virtual collaboration tools like Mural, Miro, and Jamboards allow for participation at scale, as well as the quick collection of inputs. You can use boards, like the sample below, to do a quick ethical culture survey with your team. This method could even be used as an ice breaker to get the team's input on what makes a healthy culture. This is also a means for completing a stealthy gap assessment with simultaneous participation made easy for all, and it can be achieved in a large group setting, as pair or group work, in break-out rooms, or asynchronously.

THE ART OF IDEATION

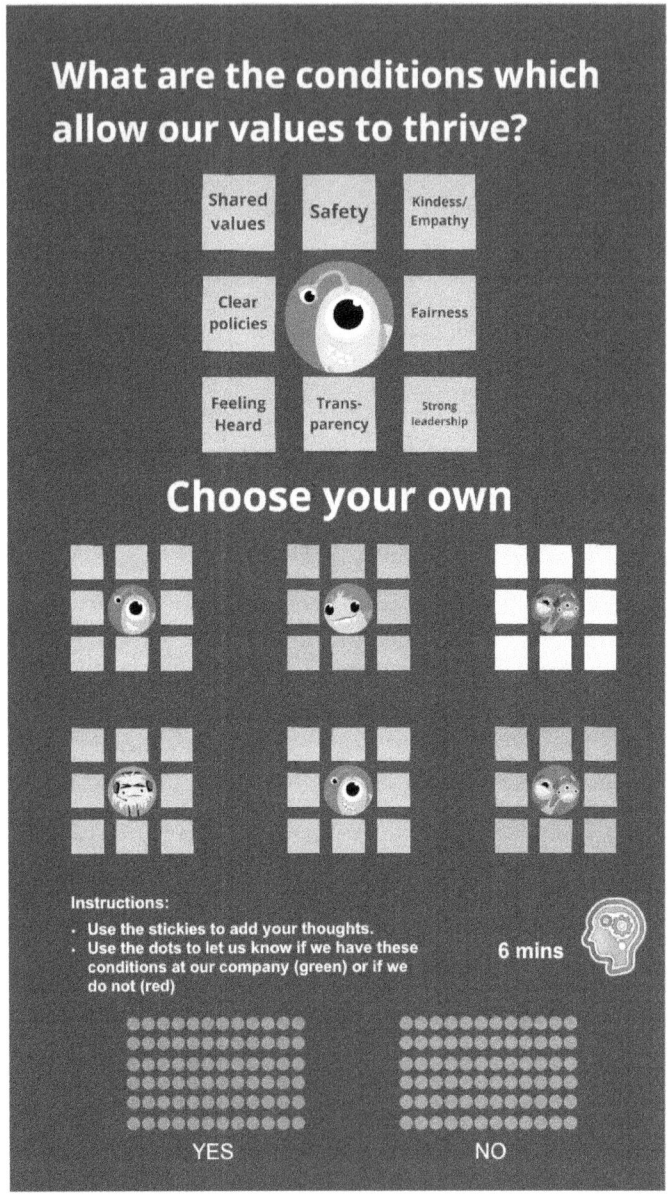

Sample Ethical Cultural Assessment for individual, pair, or break-out group work in Miro. Participants can simultaneously fill out post-its and add dots, comments, or emoticons.

Our Challenge to You

Ask yourself:

- What are your primary goals in training for culture building?
- What are the organization's key obstacles in meeting those goals or the root cause of the issues presented by not meeting those goals?
- Which of these issues can be improved through training?
- Is your training designed with the learners in mind?
- Is your training sufficiently engaging and interactive?

Consider:

- Do we have a training strategy that will close the specific gaps we have identified?
- In what ways are we leveraging stories in our training?
- What training could be enhanced with the addition of a story?
- What training could be enhanced by adding learner engagement strategies like polling, games, or giveaways?

Parting Thoughts on Training

"Tell me, and I'll forget. Teach me, and I'll remember. Involve me, and I'll learn."
– Attributed to Benjamin Franklin and Chinese Confucian philosopher

> Xun Kuang.

While training won't solve all the issues that culture builders face, it can be a high-impact tool for building both skill and awareness. Culture builders can leverage that impact by designing learning that begins with a clear purpose, and maintains focus on areas where training is most effective.

This strategic approach to learning is only the first step in ideating for training. The intentionality of the strategy might render great content, but content alone is not enough. When we partner strong content with learner engagement strategies, we are more likely to meet and even exceed our training goals.

Whether your learning platform is live, in-person, virtual, small-groups, or asynchronous modules, always consider how to involve the learner. Engagement pathways, even subtle ones, create a relationship between the learner, the content, and the teacher. That synergistic relationship produces a dynamic energy of growth and development for all.

3

Bright Ideas for Codes of Conduct

A Note from Hemma

"Ma'am, what's it like to be a woman in the army?" This was a curious, well-intentioned question from one male soldier to Roxanne, one of our guests on the *Great Women in Compliance Podcast*, an army veteran speaking in her personal capacity and recounting her time as one of the only female soldiers in a male-dominated regiment.

What struck Roxanne most about this question was that this fellow soldier wanted to do the right thing and was genuinely seeking to understand how. While soldiers sat through hours of Code training, including sexual harassment prevention training and equal opportunity training, it hadn't covered this. It was checking boxes, but it wasn't explaining the far more tricky grey area topics like how to actually be inclusive to soldiers with different experiences.

Like others in her regiment, Roxanne had no trouble remembering the lofty messages from the Code of Ethics. Still, there was often a disconnect between the calls to "respect and treat people as they should be treated" or "act with integrity" and the reality on the ground. What did these things mean? And what should that look like in practice?

The Code was well-intentioned, asking people to do the right thing, be ethical, and maintain the trust and integrity of an important institution. Clearly, the Code was addressing a relevant problem. At that time, Roxanne was reading reports of a high incidence of sexual harassment and assault in the army in the New York Times, the exact type of unethical behavior that destroys lives and erodes public trust.

Yet still, the Code and related training weren't effective in helping Roxanne, her peers, or even her superiors know how to prevent this, how to report issues, or what to do when receiving such a report. Something was lost in translation from aspiration to impact.

Roxanne saw the influence and impact of the ethical behaviors of any one particular leader on the people they led - ethical leaders could set a tone for ethical behavior. However, a leader's tolerance of problematic behaviors, even if subtle, could set that tone and culture for everyone.

Despite lofty claims of zero tolerance for retaliation, it felt like common knowledge that being seen to speak up about issues was at your peril. In some cases, references to the Code or related training were minimized and even ridiculed as a joke.

I don't know how many times Roxanne had to receive a communication addressed to her regiment that began with the word "Gentlemen" before she was moved to take action. But this was the spark for an audacious idea. Roxanne asked: What if we approached this space from the perspective of how you would design a Code intended to work rather than merely check a box? Could we intentionally bring that Code to life through practical training and tools that make reporting safe, easy, and accessible?

Roxanne decided workplace training didn't have to be boring, and administering it didn't have to be a pain. She partnered with software engineer Anne, and together, they created Ethena to bring smart technology and engaging training content to the compliance industry and focus on culture change. Their collaborative ideation resulted in a bold decision paired with action to reimagine culture building and bring aspirational Codes of Conduct to life.

Roxanne Petraeus is an army veteran, a former corporate executive at McKinsey, and an entrepreneur co-founder (with Anne Solmssen) of Ethena, a technology company that aims to build the future of ethical and inclusive workplaces.

Our Concept for Code of Conduct Ideation:

Keep your eye on the prize

Why does your Code of Conduct or Code of Ethics exist? Is it an aspirational guide to expected behaviors? Or a summary for external partners and customers interested in what the organization stands for? Is it to check a box or meet some external requirement? Or a guide to ethical decision-making for your team? It can be all of these things, but the most important audience to keep in mind when you are designing your Code is the group to whom it applies.

Even if you are following regulatory guidance or planning to share your Code as part of due diligence requests from external parties, try to unpack the spirit and intent of that external requirement or request. There's likely a common set of values and behaviors that you are trying to address through the Code. It is important enough for regulators and customers to expect one. Still, in its most basic form, it is a resource to help your teams make decisions in their everyday work and a tool to operationalize your good intentions. When you remember this, it becomes a living culture-building resource that matures with the members of the culture.

Model mutual respect and empathy

If you're committed to a Code that people will want to read, reference, or quote, consider this question, "can everyone see themselves in your Code?" A great Code has content and language that reflect the organization's values and culture. Chief Ethics Officer, Michelle Beistle says, "Codes of Conduct are foundational to fostering an ethical culture in an organization. When done well, they are the bridge between an organization's Values and Policies, providing clear standards of what it means to live the organization's Values." In terms of content, corporate Codes will likely address behavior expectations, including sections on harassment prevention, fraud, bribery and corruption, conflicts of interest, etc. But in terms of language and as a motivational behavior prompt, how does your Code leave people feeling?

Is the tone of your Code authoritarian? "Always do this, never do that, remember to …etc." This might read as though some powerful being is issuing edicts to the reader and isn't likely to inspire confidence or cooperation. By contrast, a Code that addresses people on an equal playing field and models mutual respect and empathy, "We respect one another," is more likely to leave readers with a sentiment of shared commitment and a culture of unbiased accountability.

If tone matters, so does accessibility. We mean this in every sense of the word. Do readers need dictionaries, acronym guides, or glossaries to comprehend your Code? Is it written in a way that is so simple, straightforward, and clear that it cannot be misunderstood?

Does it provide examples to bring the Code to life? Do the examples reflect people from all organizational functions, levels, and geographies so each person can see how the Code applies to them? Have you included decision trees to facilitate value-based decision-making?

Is the Code visually appealing, or does it look like any other type-heavy page in your policy manual? Can you incorporate images of what the organization and individuals value that can be added to allow the Code to feel familiar and hit home? Can the Code be effortlessly accessed online or on a mobile or smart device? Is it available in multiple languages? Are you following basic accessibility guidelines for those with vision impairment or color blindness, including providing image descriptions?

To ensure you create a Code of Conduct where everyone can see themselves, ask for feedback from select groups across your organization when building or revising your Code content. When you refresh the Code of Conduct, involve key partners, leaders, and front-line staff.

A Code should represent the values that guide the group's actions and decisions. In terms of design, tone, and content, it should model those values and remind readers of a shared sense of identity. Check with the various groups in your organization to ask how a written Code can be most useful for them. Find out which parts resonate with the audience and inspire a sense of pride and which parts might provoke a negative reaction.

Is your Code too long because you have to cover so much ground? Make the document interactive so users can quickly get to the sections they need. Adding hyperlinked icons to each page of the Code will instantly allow employees to access policies, quick guides, and relevant resources for each topic addressed in the Code of Conduct. Use QR codes, posters, or screen savers to strategically place the Code along the user's daily journey rather than making them come and look for it when needed.

Here's a Bright Idea

Codes as an agent of change

Be curious about your culture before writing an aspirational Code, indicating where you want it to be. A thoughtfully drafted ethical culture survey can help you assess your organization's values and culture, and many employee engagement surveys will give you strong clues as to employee sentiment. Ask leaders to share a single word or phrase that they would say defines the organization's values. Then, ask sample team members at all levels for their version, with an eye on psychological safety for all involved. You might use a word cloud ice-breaker where you invite group members to anonymously offer suggestions and map the most frequent responses. Equipped with this input, you can make informed choices about how to present your Code, what to prioritize, and what to highlight, whether with examples of values in action, decision trees, visuals, or reflective questions. You will also find it easier to spot conflicting messages and other gaps or impediments that can be proactively addressed.

Sample word cloud generated in freewordcloudgenerator.com

Take a walk on the creative side and create a simple marketing campaign for the Code, introducing and reintroducing it across the organization as a Code written with and for all members. Have fun with it, and prioritize key messages aligning with your vision and purpose. A key message might be: "This Code of Conduct is our commitment to one another and all those with whom we do business. This is what we expect of you and also what you can expect from us." By offering ownership to readers and providing examples of how we all work together to create the culture and operationalize the Code, culture builders can successfully bring the organization's values to life.

An image of a white starship over a black sky peppered with stars was created in Canva, evoking Star Wars vibes to inspire people to access the Code of Conduct. It can be used to create stickers, coasters, button pins, and more.

A QR code allowing users to access the Code of Conduct over a green background, with a fun reference to the R.E.S.P.E.C.T. song originally recorded by Otis Redding and made even more famous by Aretha Franklin. It can be used to create stickers, coasters, button pins, and more.

THE ART OF IDEATION

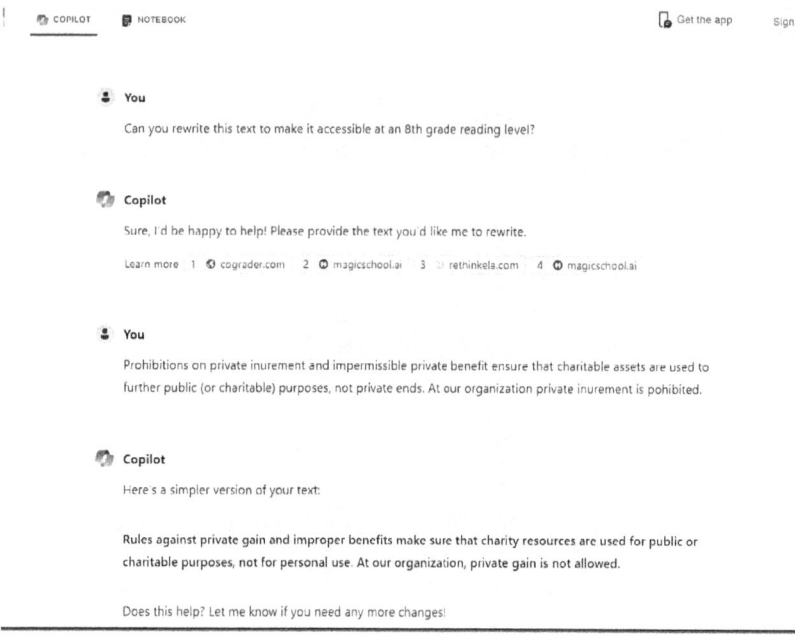

An example of a prompt in Microsoft Copilot that can adjust Code text to your preferred reading level. Be sure to consult your organization's "Acceptable uses" policies before using AI tools for your work.

Our Challenge to You

Ask yourself:

- What is the primary purpose of the Code of Conduct for my organization?
- Does the Code of Conduct align with its primary purpose?
- Is the Code of Conduct useful to leaders, teams, and individuals at your organization? If so, in what ways?
- What if the Code creates more questions than it answers? What op-

tions and strategies could you have for strengthening the guidance offered by your Code?

Consider:

- Running your Code of Conduct through a word editor to determine if it's written at an accessible reading grade level.
- Running a keyword search on your Code of Conduct to identify the primary language of the Code. This will give you an idea of the Code's underlying focus.
- Using an artificial intelligence tool like Grammarly to check the overall tone of your Code of Conduct.
- Using Adobe pdf functionality or a good website or PDF designer to make your Code interactive and mobile-friendly.

Parting thoughts on Codes of Conduct

> "Conviction is worthless unless it is converted into conduct."
> Thomas Carlyle

Rules and behavioral codes play an important role in building culture. Indeed, a culture can be defined as essentially a set of beliefs, values, principles, and guidelines that are collectively held by a group of people. With this in mind, it is important to have congruence between the sometimes aspirational convictions in the written code and any unwritten code in play that might shape behaviors and interactions within that group.

Curiosity about those unwritten codes can give you valuable insights toward creating a helpful Code that is tailored to your organization and guides behaviors representative of the culture you are building. A Code will ultimately represent your organization's good intentions. However, the culture will result from co-creating a Code over which your group members feel a shared sense of ownership and pride. Be inspired to create one that is readily accessible and easy to operationalize.

4

Bright Ideas for Influencing Leaders

A Note from Ashley

One of my favorite experiences as an operations and finance leader was my first programmatic audit. While many teams and leaders may dread an internal audit, I found the experience took my effectiveness as a leader, as well as the strength of my program, to a new level. Understanding what was important to the auditors helped me to rethink my program and improve existing systems and processes.

For years the program received compliments because of its thoroughness and practicality. Whenever anyone offered their admiration, I let them know that our magnificent system was born out of an audit we requested because we recognized that our practices could be stronger. We didn't get to that esteemed place overnight, it took honesty, humility, and help.

I've always believed that my sharpest skills and strongest learnings were born from mistakes, dead ends, and never wasting a good crisis. As a leadership coach, I was once called upon to address a group of executives after their organization experienced a crisis, and these beliefs were top of mind as I prepared my notes. The easy part of the conversation with the executives was agreeing that the crisis was bad for individuals and bad for business. We also agreed that it was important to reflect on what went wrong and to use that information to correct the course for the future.

The difficulty came when I attempted to share with the executives the role *they* could play in preventing future incidents of a similar nature. Mere minutes into this discussion, one leader stepped up abruptly to announce his views. "Look, this is too hard and not something we need to deal with at our level. Can't we just assign someone on each team to handle this type of thing?"

The executives in the room that day were experienced, smart, and capable. They were proven leaders with track records of success. I underestimated that even these accomplished leaders might feel vulnerable or uncertain when faced with a crisis. It can be especially daunting to be tasked with building the skills required for adaptive leadership, which are essential in a workplace that is always evolving.

Certainly, intelligent minds could come up with preventative, adaptive solutions for others to implement. Still, leaders cannot simply outsource the work of establishing a culture of trust and integrity. While we are all creators of the culture, the positional power afforded to leaders means they have an outsized impact on setting the tone and modeling the culture. The person with the most influence over your perceptions and experience of culture is often the one to whom you report.

As culture builders, we are often asked to prevent and detect "incidents," but we know that the next best thing when an incident sneaks up on us is to reflect and leverage the lesson toward a culture of continuous improvement. Often, an incident isn't a crisis; it is an opportunity.

With this in mind, I structured the follow-up meeting with those executives differently. While I introduced the topic, the most senior leader in the room endorsed the message by sharing a personal story that emphasized the importance of the topic. Rather than detract from the discussion, the other leaders in the room eagerly engaged and followed the example of the senior leader. Instead of carrying the integrity gospel alone, I asked a key leader to do some of the edification. In the end, the leader built trust capital, and the team gained a safe space to work on closing a skill gap.

Our Concept for Ideating to Influence Leaders

As a culture-builder in your organization, you already stand out as a leader. However, if you were solely responsible for creating and managing the culture within your organization, you wouldn't get very far in your efforts. Leaders set the tone for the organization, which involves influencing other leaders and recognizing the impact those in leadership can have on the culture.

Influencing leaders to build culture can be a massive challenge. To help, consider what matters to the various leaders at your organization. Are they concerned about employee performance, customer satisfaction, or their own ability to build trust? Whatever it is, you can tie culture building and ethical leadership to their most desired outcomes. This is how you will best influence your leaders; you must create value and benefit where they need it most. Help them succeed at something they already want to do.

Leaders often have an extensive workload and competing issues to manage. On one hand, it is easy to suggest that nothing is as important as an organization's culture, but it is all too easy to get swept up in what appear to be other pressing matters. Approaching your fellow leaders with awareness of their priorities can make you a valued strategic partner, viewed as someone who understands them and can assist them in solving their toughest problems.

A Leader's preference: do it yourself, do it with you, or done for you?

Once you've established the importance of ethical leadership, other leaders in your organization will likely need help understanding what it looks like in action.

Figure out their preferred method for receiving support. Do they want to do it themselves, be coached or guided through it, or do they want it done for them? Create tools, templates, and other resources that match their style and make it easy for all leaders to participate in culture building. Schedule prompts and set reminders for leaders. Motivate them with friendly competition or recognition. Consider tying performance incentives to demonstrable ethical leadership.

Do you want them to encourage their teams to complete the annual training? Write the key messages in bullet form, share a template email with the essential details, create a funny reminder meme that they can forward, or send a virtual Post-it note that allows them to support the message easily. This range of "prompt" to "plug and play" options can be created for your most important requests of leaders.

Make resources and techniques available that leaders can easily access online or print and keep near at hand during virtual meetings and one-on-one conversations. Provide language for leaders to share in their email signatures, newsletters, blogs, or team meetings that acknowledges the courage required to speak up and an invitation to use the Hotline or come to them directly for questions, concerns, or support.

Want leaders to encourage a speak-up culture? Remind them that most employees prefer to speak up to their local leader over every other reporting pathway. Empower them with quick guides on the basics of hearing and receiving a concern as a compassionate first responder with care and empathy. Katherine Manning, in her book *The Empathetic Workplace: 5 Steps to a Compassionate, Calm, and Confident Response to Trauma on the Job*, shares an easy-to-remember "LASER technique" for just this purpose that could be the basis of a resource kit on this topic for leaders.

Here's a Bright Idea

While leaders are often highly talented, the most talented know they aren't naturally skilled in every arena. Building and maintaining a healthy culture requires adaptive learning. As culture builders, we can help leaders become ambassadors of the culture by offering simple, practical pathways to create and uphold trust and integrity.

Using a tool card like the sample below, you might provide nudges to leaders to engage them in inspiring ways to build the culture you desire through ethical leadership.

Simple Ways for Leaders to Build Trust through Ethical Leadership

- Invite people to raise concerns: listen without judgement, appreciate the courage it takes to speak up, take action toward resolution.

- Center the person impacted before correcting wrong information, defending, or reacting to feedback/concerns.

- Talk about organizational Values and the Code of Conduct.

- Celebrate when folks do the right thing.

- Align your decisions and behavior with your Values.

- Share stories from life, books, movies, or television that shaped your Values.

- Highlight a helpful tool or quick guide that can build awareness of key policies and procedures on your team.

- Prioritize compliance training and discuss it with your team.

A sample tool card created in Canva, listing simple ways for leaders to build trust through ethical leadership.

You could replace "build trust" in the title with the culture initiative most valued by leadership at your organization. For example:

- Simple Ways for Leaders to **Improve Employee Engagement** through Ethical Leadership
- Simple Ways for Leaders to **Create Psychological Safety** through Ethical Leadership
- Simple Ways for Leaders to **Build a Speak-Up Culture** through Ethical Leadership
- Simple Ways for Leaders to **Reduce Burnout and Improve Retention** through Ethical Leadership

Consider developing a virtual toolkit for leaders that offers examples of incorporating integrity in their daily work and spark conversations. This might look like organizing content by topic in a catalog of plug-and-play tools, from template emails to funny cartoons to quotes from the Code that could help teams navigate dilemmas and establish norms.

The toolkit could provide ideas for incorporating these tools in emails, newsletters, one-on-one discussions, performance reviews, training, or retreats. When you know your audience well, you can tailor the tools to meet the most pressing needs of the leaders and design products to appeal to the general culture of the organization. Leaders are more likely to share quotes, cartoons, and the like that are on-brand for the mission and truly reflect the value and importance of the work their teams are engaged in at the organization.

These efforts don't have to stop with the catalog. Strategically share your best tools during leadership meetings, coordinating with the season to build value in the product. For example, share quick guides and talking points around electioneering during election season. As you approach the holidays, share entertaining cartoons that build awareness around gift giving and receiving or responsible alcohol use at company events. Leaders who enjoy the content are often excited to share it with their larger teams.

Don't forget your middle managers and the pivotal leadership role they play in your culture. Interactions with a person's direct supervisor can make or break an individual employee's experience of your culture. The fabulous team at Ethico, led by brothers Nick Gallo and Giovanni Gallo, put together a comprehensive Middle Managers Toolkit to empower people managers to lead with empathy and drive compliance. It is available on their website at ethico.com. Resources like this can be a great source of inspiration as you consider how best to equip your leaders for success.

> **Important Reminders:**
>
> - You can do anything
> - You are doing great
> - You are amazing
> - The Annual Compliance Training window closes on April 17th
> - You are valued

A friendly flyer made with Canva could nudge team members to complete their annual compliance training by the deadline.

Leaders are busy - lean into this as an opportunity to ideate

As a culture builder, you cannot shy away from influencing leaders, even though they likely have executive support teams who will guard their calendars like a vault. It is precisely because these leaders can be too busy and focused on their own priorities that you will have to find creative ways to spur their engagement and motivate them to be ambassadors for the cause.

Kristy Grant-Hart invites us to be unafraid of bigger and harder problems because that's precisely when you might come up with more exciting solutions. In her book *Your Year as a Wildly Effective Compliance Officer*, Kristy explains how "constraints breed creativity." She invites us to consider how we would rise to the occasion if additional obstacles, like an accelerated deadline or a budget cut in half, came our way. If you are forced to find leaner, more inspiring, and more effective ways to influence leaders with limited capacity or willingness for engagement, the resulting ideation might be just the rocket fuel you need to influence a culture breakthrough.

Our Challenge to You

Ask yourself:

- How can you leverage the unique positional power of your leaders to model ethical decision-making?
- Are there opportunities to make compliance and risk management a standard part of goal setting or opportunity planning?
- How can leaders operationalize their good intentions?
- What resources can you provide as a toolkit for ethical leadership?
- What resources can you provide as a toolkit for culture building?

Consider:

- Providing leaders with on-brand materials they will proudly share as their own in their live, asynchronous, and fixed communications.
- Reframing your approach to a busy or reluctant leader and using their circumstances to inspire broader creative ideation.

Parting Thoughts on Influencing Leaders

> "The only thing of real importance that leaders do is to create and manage culture."
> – Edgar Schein

It sounds provocative, but Edgar Schein may have been onto something when he spoke of the role of leaders in creating and managing culture. Even if it isn't the only thing of real importance that leaders do, it is certainly high up there, and the benefits of doing this well will positively impact their ability to achieve other goals.

If you are reading this book and identify as a culture builder, it is likely because you are already a leader, notwithstanding your title or hierarchical position in the organization. One of your opportunities is to influence and create other leaders who will co-create and manage the culture with you. This journey will only be enhanced by creative crowdsourcing and peer ideation to discover how to do that well.

5

Bright Ideas for Artificial Intelligence

A Note from Ashley

Recently, my teenage daughter was asked to craft a persuasive essay for a school assignment. While proud of her essay, she was furious when she learned that another student used an AI tool, ChatGPT, to complete the assignment. To add insult to injury, the teacher was so impressed with the friend's, … er …, AI's essay that he read it to the class as a shining example of a well-composed persuasive essay.

Ever the justice-seeker, my daughter confronted her friend about using an AI tool not only to complete an assignment but to accept recognition for the accomplishment. Of course, the friend shrugged and said she wasn't losing any sleep over the decision.

For days, my daughter stomped around the house, proclaiming the evils of AI. In one hilarious moment, she stopped me in the kitchen to declare, "I really hate AI, mom!" To this declaration, I responded that she did not hate AI, in fact, she uses and enjoys AI daily. She realized that her frustrations weren't with AI but with what she perceived as its unethical use.

Undoubtedly, this is something we are all grappling with as professionals. Not only are we charged with helping to figure out the ethical standard for AI use in our organizations, but there is something else we may also be feeling when it comes to artificial intelligence - threatened.

For some, this feeling is born from a sense of overwhelm by the rapid presence of AI in our world. It's literally everywhere. Ask your phone a question, AI responds. Thinking about investing, AI is shouting for your attention. Applying for a new job, AI is likely deciding whether or not your resume makes it to someone's inbox. Enjoying a social media post? Well, AI probably wrote that, drew that, posted that, and maybe even made that up. If you feel like you're drowning in AI and aren't sure how to board this seemingly *Terminator*-esque bandwagon, you aren't alone.

For others, the threat is more personal. If you're like me, you may feel like you're competing with AI. For my entire career, I have often served as the creative thinker, the wordsmith, and the outliner of the team's vision. Now, everyone has these skills at their fingertips. Might AI render us obsolete?

We could take that stance and try to fight the advent of AI with all of our human energy, but we would inevitably lose. We can't possibly hold back the tidal wave that is AI. However, we can harness its power to up our potential, work faster and smarter, and maybe even enjoy our work more. If I were given a choice between presenting bright ideas or monitoring expense reports, you could always put your money on my preference to present the former. The good news is that not only can AI help me outline my expense report presentation, create exciting graphics, and review my tone - but it might also have the ability to help me monitor expense reports more quickly and more thoroughly.

Certainly, we must employ AI ethically, and if we are tasked with setting that standard, it pays to be versed in AI's offerings, business potential, and inevitable evolution.

Our Concept for Artificial Intelligence Ideation

AI is the here and now, and culture builders will be involved in defining responsible use and deftly leveraging AI to identify risk, detect wrongdoing, and prevent harm. Given our roles, it can be tempting to focus more on AI risk than on how AI is the future of our work. However, the only reason there is an imperative to talk about AI risk is to unlock the vast opportunity of AI responsibly and to help us do hard things well.

It can be uncomfortable, intimidating, and somewhat overwhelming for the uninitiated. Wherever you find yourself, consider your potential role in what is becoming known as the fourth industrial revolution as someone who can unlock this opportunity for your stakeholders. The only way to get to responsible AI as a culture builder is to take your place on the innovation express train and co-create the future.

To start, we offer baby steps for incorporating the power of AI to get work done. However, we will also entertain and explore the immense possibilities that exist for all of us as culture builders.

Start to experiment within your current risk tolerance

Have you ever received draft language for a policy, Code of Ethics, training, or general update that required several readings to grasp? Imagine all those employees who do not work in compliance or legal, tasked with interpreting and adopting the guidance set forth by these documents. We talk a lot about accessibility, and for good reason. If we want a policy to be adopted, training to be effective, or a Code to be motivating, it MUST be easy to read, comprehend, and commit to memory so that it drives the desired behaviors.

A simple way to leverage AI to get you there is to check your document's grade level or reading ease. You might use AI tools like Grammarly, which can give you feedback on your tone, spelling, and grammar. Word processing tools have evolved significantly beyond the now-retired Clippy, a friendly if slightly distracting, virtual paperclip assistant that appeared in Microsoft Office in the 1990s. You can now use the Editor tool to assess the readability of a Microsoft Word document. The AI-powered Editor offers a Flesch-Kincade readability score and reading level, an inclusive language assessment, and general refinement ideas. You can click on each refinement area and be directed to any potentially problematic words or phrases in your document. Granted, there will be some things you can ignore according to preference, but generally, this can be a simple, helpful, accessible review step.

We should aim to reduce complexity to make reading more enjoyable and accessible for all readers. For universal readability, a preteen reading level (age 12-14) is recommended. That translates to a Flesch-Kincaid 8th-grade reading level target for broad audiences. Remember, in any jurisdiction, if your reader needs 16 years of education or higher, you've got a painfully narrow window of accessibility. The authors checked this chapter's current version in the Editor tool and found it could use some work. It is at a reading level of 11.2 and a readability score of 49 - acceptable for a professional audience but with room for improvement.

Build your muscles in readiness for the opportunities

As an initial reaction to the increased availability of AI tools, many organizations implemented strict acceptable use policies limiting the use of AI tools, no doubt on the sage advice of their legal and compliance teams. We know to check our sources, avoid sharing proprietary and confidential information, use disclaimers when a tool is in pre-release testing or beta mode, and keep the human in the loop to check for accuracy and AI hallucinations (that mystical thing that happens sometimes, where the AI makes something up, but it sounds like a fact or appears to be a valid source).

However, with the appropriate mitigation in place, including internal or proprietary instances of AI tools that don't share information outside of the organization, exciting opportunities are out there. With secure, well-vetted tools, teams could use AI to start a draft investigation plan or create a draft investigation report. Teams could enter key prompts and have AI build interesting stories for training and engagement. If you need to get a first draft of a policy, an SOP, a set of team norms, or safety guidelines, AI can help you start. AI can create logos, imagery, infographics, or even outline suggested strategic plans for your team. The possibilities are endless.

AI won't replace you, but it might enhance or accelerate the things you are already doing or kick-start the things for which you are seeking inspiration. Consider if AI can help improve the quality of your drafts for style, tone, or readability. AI tools can give you a jump start from the blank page so you can have a suggested outline or starting point and then focus on building out your desired content, reviewing and editing, and having more time for the tasks that bring you joy.

Image generated with the Photoleap application and altered in Canva to convey a tailored message.

An "ethical hero" inspired by Hemma's headshot

An "ideator" inspired by Ashley's headshot

Images generated using iPhone photos and the PhotoLeap Application.

Strategies for responsible use and design

Do you have a strategy for the responsible use of AI by your team? Have you converted this into a policy and a governance framework for monitoring that policy, and enforcing it? In this time of fast-paced regulation and innovation, companies are taking several approaches. Let's call them the bear, the hare, and the tortoise - and be honest that the race is on, and the winner has not yet been called.

The bear is in their cave - in a holding pattern, call it hibernation, feeling like it is not quite the right season to come out with a strategy or policy. Indeed, it seems like every day, a new treaty, regulation, standard, principle, or rule around AI is promulgated, and there will be much more to learn. It can be tempting to lie in wait and leave the decision on whether to move your resources on this effort to later.

The hare is decisive and ready to race ahead; they have already published an AI policy and may already be on later iterations. Some hares have quickly decided to shut it down or severely limit uses for fear of vulnerabilities and unmitigated risk. These hares might now be spending their time grappling with enforcing this policy, but they may have to run around and start the race again at some point. Others have fully embraced the revolution, encouraging responsible experimentation with available tools, and looking for ways to build ethical design into their product lines. They are fully engaged and are looking well beyond the finish line.

The tortoise is taking a more steady approach in the race. They keep moving forward but are not over-indexing on effort or resources. The tortoises aren't the first movers, but they are willing to look around and learn from others in the race.

Wherever you find yourself in this race, you will set the pace according to your culture. From another lens, you may also be setting the tone for your culture according to the approach you take. None of us want to be caught off-guard like a "deer in headlights."

An image of an animated bear, a hare, a tortoise, and a deer, generated by Microsoft Designers AI image generation tool with the following prompt: "A hare and a tortoise in a race with a sleeping bear in a cave."

For those of you who have responsible AI policies or acceptable use policies in place, check if your policy is still fit for purpose. Even though the ink may still feel wet on that policy, this is one to watch regularly to ensure it continues to make sense for your teams. "Approved uses" lists may also need to be updated regularly. For example, a policy that bans the use of non-approved AI for work will become problematic as more of our daily productivity tools launch AI features and functionality, e.g., word processing, recruiting tools, video calling and note-takers, and navigation systems.

Avoid publishing a restrictive policy that everyone will inadvertently be breaching on day one. Instead, discover what opportunities might exist for your teams with AI and co-create feasible risk mitigation strategies. For example, consider making it easy for team members to identify proprietary and confidential information rather than simply banning all uses of AI tools.

For those of you who are including AI in your product design, check on your team's shared understanding of what ethical or responsible AI can mean. If you are using AI or Large Language Models to drive efficiencies and productivity and 'learn' from existing data sets, develop practices to ensure you check the sources and integrity of that data. Think of the adage garbage in, garbage out (GIGO). Crowdsource risk intelligence here by involving your business teams and partners, including IT, data management, and product teams, especially if you work somewhere where your teams are ideating and innovating on the development and commercial uses of AI.

A culture of innovation requires experimentation and psychological safety around mistakes. It can also benefit from transparency. For example, the head of an engineering department opened a Slack channel asking all employees to share how they were using AI within the company's proprietary instance of ChatGPT.

This channel became a hub of ideation and innovation as the company crowdsourced its employees' creativity, productivity, and efficiency hacks. It generated some friendly competition between teams as it tracked who was using it most and for what. And it provided some excellent data for those teams charged with the company's AI strategy. The ethics and compliance team pinned their principle-based policy on AI uses to the channel for all users to consult easily. This small act of creating a space and permission to experiment created a powerful micro-culture of trust and collective ideation. Undoubtedly, it roused a few sleeping bears and teased them out of their caves.

Here's a Bright Idea

What if the thing we want to do is already being done in another domain? What if that technology already exists? In any customer-facing organization, prioritizing the customer experience (CX) is critical, and measuring customer sentiment can help you keep track. The same applies to every member of the culture you are building. Simon Sinek has been quoted as saying, "Happy employees ensure happy customers. And happy customers ensure happy shareholders—in that order." It stands to reason that culture building is not just about your customer— or shareholder-facing approach but also very much about the employee experience (EX) and sentiment.

The good news is that when focusing on the internal employee or team culture in an organization, we can learn a lot from customer relationship management and customer satisfaction scoring (CSAT). Modern customer relationship management technology and CX tooling have been built for this purpose: to provide answers quickly, obtain relevant data from customers, and automate repetitive processes with ease.

AI has been leveraged to provide agents with information at their fingertips, unlocking operational agility and reducing response times. AI has enabled agent-less interactions through AI-powered bots, which can quickly assess user intent, exchange relevant information, gauge customer sentiment and satisfaction, crowdsource feedback or other intelligence, instantly mine existing data to predict and store customer preferences and behaviors, and much much more.

In Chapter 7, we will share more ideas on leveraging AI to crowd-source intelligence. But it is worth paying attention to how AI is being used every day to influence culture in other spaces. Mine these examples as sources of inspiration and ideate by asking, "What if we could apply that to our culture-building efforts?"

Using Generative AI tools built on your company's culture and policy documents can get answers quickly into the hands of your end users instead of making them manually sift through your vast banks of content or policy. This is one way to show you mean what you say when you have a culture of kindness, empathy, and innovation. The same technology can prompt ethical behaviors with just-in-time reminders and other regular interactions while simultaneously providing access to the relevant processes and controls. Inspiration is everywhere, and the possibilities abound.

Our Challenge to You

Ask yourself:

- Can AI tools help you solve an existing problem?

- Do you have an acceptable use policy that covers AI?
- Is your responsible AI-acceptable use policy still fit for purpose?
- How is AI being used to improve elements of culture in other domains, and could this be applied to your domain?
- If you want to build a culture of innovation, what would that look like?

Consider:

- Asking AI to outline a policy you've been tasked with writing.
- Asking AI to write a story by feeding it prompts that determine the length of the story, the type of issue (conflicts of interest, bribery, fraud), the type of character (a manager, a senior leader, a new employee), and the industry (healthcare, environmental, finance, technology).
- Asking AI to generate an image or clip art that is tailored to a presentation, meme, or announcement you hope to deliver soon.
- Asking AI to teach you how to do something e.g. How do I outline an investigative report? How do I write a Code of Conduct? How do I build training on gift giving and receiving?
- Asking AI to teach you how to make the best use of AI for your function.

Parting Thoughts on Artificial Intelligence

"Some people call this artificial intelligence, but the reality is this technology will enhance us. So instead of artificial intelligence, I think we'll augment

our intelligence."
– Virginia "Ginni" Rometty, former CEO of IBM

Whether your attitudes around AI resemble our bear, hare, or tortoise characters, you can leverage the idea-enhancing power of AI to build culture. With the ability to sort and interpret data, solve problems, automate tasks, and fill in gaps, AI as a resource should not be neglected. Already leveraged by nearly every industry, it has claimed a prominent role in the future of work.

It's normal to feel uncertain or even intimidated by AI. However, you're likely already utilizing AI in your everyday life and gradually acclimating to its presence. We encourage you to lean in, learn more, and expand your understanding and use of AI. With the benefit of that knowledge and experience, you will not only be a more effective culture builder, but you will also be able to lead the conversation about the ethical use of AI.

Should you feel diminished by the possibilities and uncertainties of an AI future, consider the thoughts of Ginni Rometty. Perhaps our work as culture builders can be enhanced and our talents augmented by the ever-ready help-meet of Artificial Intelligence.

6

Bright Ideas for Investigations

A Note from Hemma

"Things really changed since the beginning of the investigation." I blinked twice at the text. Wait, what did he mean? I was doing a welfare check with one of our employees who had raised concerns about aspects of the office culture. I was already feeling bad, the investigation was taking much longer than I had hoped. Between personnel changes in the employee relations team and a new outside counsel, I had a sinking feeling in the pit of my stomach that the people who were brave enough to speak up about an issue on their team may have lost all hope in us. One part of me wanted to sink into the shadows, knowing I couldn't control how quickly these other teams could close on this investigation, despite the fact that I was, to all intents and purposes, accountable as the face of compliance and the guardian of the hotline.

I shook it off and decided to at least control what I could and do the next right thing—a simple wellness check-in with the employees. This was a chance to iterate our gratitude for speaking up and a request to bear with us. But those words, now flashing across the screen, made me wonder if, in this time that the team was left waiting, we had left space for the next worst thing - retaliation for speaking up.

I think about retaliation a lot, in part because I like to keep my commitments, and at the end of every policy I have written, I have promised our employees that we take retaliation seriously and have a zero-tolerance policy. I braced myself and watched the three dots on the message in anticipation to see what was coming next: "Everything is different."

Different? I perked up and texted back with a glimmer of hope and asked tentatively, "Have they changed for the better?"

The reply came quickly: "A lot better."

The relief was palpable, and now curiosity rose in my chest.

"I am so glad." I replied, "We like to leave space for people to recover where possible. I am really happy to hear you are seeing a difference."

He replied. "I am. The whole team is. Thank you for that."

My curiosity peaked. What could have happened that allowed the office culture to improve so rapidly, even during an investigation? Whatever it was, to the degree we influenced it as a compliance function, we wanted to be able to repeat it.

Before you read on, have a think and try to list 10 things that you could do during an investigation that would help initiate immediate improvements in the culture. Even if your hunch is that the people involved must have shown incredible maturity, leadership, and emotional intelligence - what could you do to ensure the conditions are ripe for such positive reparative behaviors?

In this case, we retraced our steps to look for the recipe. Here is some of what we found:

The ingredients:

A ladle of radical empathy, curiosity, and compassion. This is for all participants in the investigation - those who felt they were impacted by or witnessed harmful behaviors, for the wider team and first responders, and those who are alleged to have been responsible for those behaviors.

A healthy serving of grace and respect. Even without knowing what happened and the outcome of the investigation, we took a human-centered approach, seeking to understand, instead of leading with judgment or disappointment, with express acknowledgment that regardless of the outcome, this is stressful for all parties, and that together, we can do a hard thing well.

A dash of transparency. Be open about the investigative process, your goals and how you plan to get there, the limitations of the process, and manage expectations for the timeline, confidentiality, retaliation, and other matters. Check in and stay in touch with stakeholders so they aren't left in the dark, even if it is merely to say sorry that it is taking a little longer than anticipated.

Ample gratitude for the courage and cooperation of all parties

involved. Thank all participants, including those under investigation, and remind them that they are helping everyone and the company by showing up for this process.

The instructions:

Show a willingness to take accountability. What could the company or the service functions (leadership, compliance, HR, etc.) do better to help avoid the conditions that might have led to this situation? If your training isn't really hitting the mark for this situation, own that, take feedback, and make a commitment to change this. Be curious and look to see if the organization is inadvertently incentivizing poor choices with our tone from the top. Take any reasonable immediate or interim mitigation steps that are objectively identified as necessary without waiting for a determination on who may have done what.

Be clear and unapologetic with all parties and the broader team about the culture you want and each team member's role as a creator of the culture and not merely a consumer.

Be inspiring and empowering, not patronizing. Manage expectations and support rather than co-opt the healing and reparation journey. Remind participants that the measure of us is how we respond and react in these moments rather than what might have come before. Encourage participants to project into the future and consider how their future selves would be proud of how they are showing up in this challenging situation.

Be curious as to what else might be true, and seek input from the whole team as to how to pro-actively create the environments where we can all thrive. Look for the information behind the emotions.

Never waste a good crisis. Ask for input on concrete and practical lessons learned *as part of the investigative interviews* and consider ways to apply those lessons for the benefit of other teams in the company. Curiosity and intention around these things, as a systematic part of the investigative process, can go a long way to building trust and leaving space for recovery, even before you receive the final investigative report.

Our Concept for Investigations Ideation

Part of culture-building is enforcing the community codes and conducting fair investigations into alleged incidents that go against those codes. Solid investigations require solid procedures. Culture professionals need to be adept at writing and adhering to a robust set of investigation protocols and guidelines. Such guidelines should provide guarantees of fairness, consistency, and direction and can build trust in the investigative process. And, like many written policies, they will only get you so far.

To promote ultimate trust in the investigation process, you must embrace a human approach to your work within the guideposts of your established processes. This means approaching every interviewee with care, compassion, and respect, including the person or persons accused of wrongdoing. It means staying curious and empathetic as you listen and learn from those involved in the investigation, with continual awareness of the impact on culture and an openness to opportunities for remediation.

Compassionate communication can exist alongside accountability, coaching, and even disciplinary action. It's essential to manage investigations with care for the teams and individuals impacted. Minimize disruption with a solid investigation plan in place before interviews begin. Be thoughtful about power dynamics and the potential impact of participation on individuals. It's easy to manage what you choose to share during interviews, but also consider what you didn't share that might be important for participants to hear. Offer expectations about the timeline and who they can contact if anything changes or they need support. Talk openly about the process, and be sure to discuss the nuance.

Pursuing organic solutions can minimize the risk of retaliation and team disruption, result in more feasible recommendations, and increase the possibility of adherence to the same. One way to do this is by asking those interviewed what they hope to see as an outcome of this investigation. Consider asking this of all participants, not just the reporter. This question allows the investigator to gauge the information or triggers behind the emotions and the significance of the impact on each person. The investigator can seek to understand what beliefs, whether true or not, participants might hold about the investigation and potential outcomes. It also allows the investigator to see how closely aligned participants are in their expectations.

Investigators might discover that the reporter feels confident addressing the issue independently after being empowered with knowledge of their rights and available avenues of redress. This could look like a team member bringing new policy information to light, helping redirect a project, sharing the impacts with other participants, engaging bystanders, and simply requesting a change in behaviors.

In some cases, investigators might discover a gulf between those involved, and much more discovery is needed to develop effective recommendations while thinking about how best to close the gap. Here is where ideation comes into its own, and we can bring in support to figure out how to do a hard thing well.

Here's a Bright Idea

Investigations are emotional experiences that trigger all sorts of fears and insecurities in the participants. When you talk about an investigative process, it pays to approach each communication with this in mind. How you handle your reporting channels and investigations, and the way the members of your organization perceive that, is an important factor in your culture.

Consider proactively using transparency around the investigative process. This means sharing with participants what to expect to increase trust between potential reporters, witnesses, and the investigative teams.

Deal with the elephants in the room. Employees might have fear or reservations about the investigation process. They may be influenced by organizational myths that reports aren't taken seriously, that the company will protect itself first and brush things under the carpet, or that policies are rarely enforced.

Share anonymized data to bust those organizational myths. Reporting openly about hotline trends and investigation outcomes demonstrates that the company has robust processes and practices to manage concerns that are raised. This practice also raises awareness about the types of reports raised around the organization and the multitude of pathways for managing the outcomes of investigations, from counseling to organizational adjustment and learning, all the way to disciplinary action and termination.

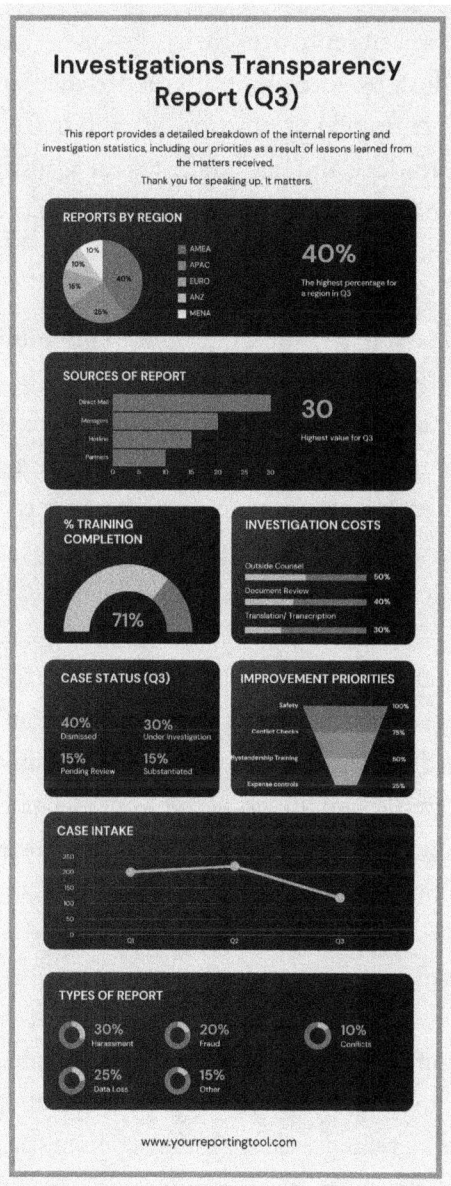

Sample Investigations Transparency report created in Canva with illustrative data to give examples of what might be shared to build trust through transparency.

Culture builders can enhance their resources, messaging, and awareness-building by leveraging the experience and feedback of partners outside their field or function, like internal communications team members, leaders, and field staff. It's especially helpful to have others review written materials and other communications that detail the reporting process and Hotline to staff.

It's possible that while we often effectively communicate the basics of the investigation process, someone from a different team may notice that the most critical messaging about investigations is missing. Overuse of legal terms and austere language will not offer the clarity most people desire. It is easy for subject matter experts and professionals to get lost in their own deep understanding of the nuances and fail to clearly and selectively communicate to broader audiences.

Convert your guidance to infographics, process charts, and videos, and then review them with a trusted partner to ensure you have accessible language that will not lend itself to confusion or misunderstanding. Consider if examples might be helpful and be transparent about the reality and nuance that exists within the investigation process. Those nuances can offer clarity and build trust because they manage expectations and allow participants to understand the process in a deeper and more meaningful way.

Reporters will appreciate an acknowledgment that delay can be frustrating when explaining a new setback or backlog. Undoubtedly, people will experience increased ease with the reporting and investigation experience after reviewing clear, thoughtful, accessible, human-first materials that acknowledge their diverse perspectives and the broader context (including their hope, courage, insecurity, frustration, and fear).

A sample infographic made in Canva addresses key knowledge needs for employees who want to know more about the reporting process.

Our Challenge to You

Ask Yourself:

- What guidance exists to inform staff and leaders about the investigation process at your organization?
- Is that guidance easy to find?
- Is that guidance easy to understand for a non-legal or compliance professional?
- Are you using unexplained acronyms.
- Have you included words that may not be intuitive outside of compliance (subject, process leader, triage, etc).
- Is the information provided still accurate? Have your practices evolved since the information was published?
- What barriers make it difficult for employees to speak up at your organization?
- Are those barriers addressed clearly in your investigation process information?

Consider:

- In what ways can we expressly acknowledge the toll an investigation can take on all parties involved and mitigate that even during the investigation?
- How would you want a loved one to be treated at work if they were part of a workplace investigation?
- What is the best outcome we can expect from any particular compliance or HR investigation? How can we move towards that?
- What options are there for greater transparency about the investigations and outcomes while maintaining the integrity of the investigation and appropriate confidentiality for all parties?

Parting Thoughts on Investigations

> "What are facts but compromises? A fact merely marks the point where we have agreed to let investigation cease."
> – Bliss Carman

Organizational investigations are helpful far beyond determining whether the particular allegations of wrongdoing are substantiated. The mere act of deciding to start an investigation brings integrity to the codes and policies you are trying to enforce. A robust and transparent investigation process, which manages expectations and shows that reporting isn't futile but genuinely appreciated, will do more for your speak-up culture than any campaign.

Moreover, an investigation can give deep insights into the conditions in which your teams work, including the behaviors, underlying triggers, reactions, and how people respond when things go wrong. It is an opportune moment to positively influence behavior, reset, and leave spaces to recover. By showing that the investigation process has helped you learn and improve things for everyone, you set the actual bar for the behaviors you will and will not tolerate. This practice of upholding shared values and striving for continuous improvement will, in turn, shape the culture.

7

Bright Ideas for Crowdsourcing Intelligence

A Note from Hemma

Can I park here? I always try to arrive early when I drive into Washington, DC, and my lifelong knack for finding a car parking space right outside my intended destination never fails me. But once I have deftly maneuvered my car into an impossibly small space, I immediately second-guess myself. Can I actually park here? One glimpse at the nearest signpost is enough to know that you can never be too sure in the city. Isn't this compliance gone wrong. On the one hand, I am impressed that each 'department' of the municipal parking authority has managed to condense their specific rule onto a small sign. But I am in equal parts exasperated that they couldn't have done more to work together and give me more instant peace of mind. I just want to know if I can park in that spot, at that time, on that day, and quickly.

A picture of a set of Washington, D.C. parking signs from Reddit.

Enter technology. You only have to get it wrong a couple of times - whether making yourself late or paying a parking fine, to search for another way.

Thanks to a helpful sticker on a parking meter, I discovered the Parkmobile application, which knows where I am by virtue of a Global Positioning System (GPS) and can instantly confirm where I can park via my handheld device. It also allows me to pay by phone when needed. A friend told me about the SpotHero app, which helps me find garage parking with available spaces near my destination and even pay ahead to have extra peace of mind and keep me moving forward. The navigation application Waze helps me plan to arrive on time, choose the best route, avoid traffic, and get just-in-time alerts about obstacles in the road or speed traps based on the inputs of other drivers who have taken that route minutes before me. It will even warn me if I am driving through an accident hotspot. The technology is helping us *crowdsource risk intelligence,* and get relevant risk mitigation knowledge into the hands of those who need it, when they need it, for their own unique journey.

This inspired two inquiries on how to do the same for the employees we serve as a corporate ethics and compliance function. First, how do we get fast and relevant answers into these employees' hands so they can keep moving forward to their own unique destination? We want our information to bring clarity, not confusion; ease, and peace of mind, not frustration or panic. Second, how do we crowdsource from those same employees the most relevant risk and mitigation ideas to collect pertinent data and keep all of us moving forward?

A risk assessment should be continuous rather than a one-off or annual process—which resides mainly in the files of the compliance team—and should ideally leverage the eyes, ears, and insights of those operationalizing the companies' goals and involve those with a unique vantage point to identify potential and actual vulnerabilities and alternative routes.

Despite our best intentions here, the elephant in the room is that we don't feel equipped to complete this process more than once a year, and then, only barely scratching the surface of what the risks might be at any one time. To make things harder, each employee is on a unique journey, on a specific path, with a specific destination, on a specific day, at a particular time. Any mass communication on policy or compliance will feel irrelevant to most. It doesn't matter how often you might tell me that the street cleaning restriction on Martin Luther King Boulevard is on Tuesday morning; I will be unlikely to digest that information until I need parking in that area on a Tuesday morning. We also know that rules and risks can fluctuate depending on location, time of day, etc.

As far as meeting the company's business objectives, many will be heading to the same or similar "destination" and experiencing the same risks and rules. Along that journey, they are more likely to be exposed to pertinent information and experience with relevant risks and the best ways to mitigate them. How can we bring to our work the magic of applications like Waze that have made it easy for users to crowdsource and share that information in real-time for the benefit of all other users?

This reflective inquiry had us thinking about how to design and build our programs and interactions around the user or employee experience (UX/ EX). Our goal is to map out their journey, understand why they are on that journey and what they want to achieve, and ensure we have useful and relevant resources available to help them keep moving forward with ease and peace of mind. We also wanted to find easy ways for them to leverage their vantage point and share back helpful information with others on that route. In this way, we aspired to get people where they wanted to go, safely and lawfully, confident in their ability to make ethical decisions along the way, and unlocking safe and responsible journeys and growth as a service.

Our Concept for Crowdsourcing Intelligence Ideation

It's not uncommon for opportunity and risk assessments to be tasks completed at a high level within the organization through interviews or questionnaires for senior leaders. However, a wealth of information in every function, geography, and tier of any organization can be leveraged to understand these key opportunities and the attending risks more accurately. The concept of crowdsourcing risk intelligence is an acknowledgment that leadership doesn't have a monopoly on the perspectives we need, and we should find creative ways to capture the vantage point of all members of the culture we are trying to create.

Whether through surveys and questionnaires, focus groups and interviews, or town halls, it is important to open up listening channels for those most impacted by the culture. People will feel seen, heard, and valued, and most importantly respected.

Inspired by the brilliant ideators who keep us moving forward on the roads, we decided to experiment by applying some of the same principles to the corporate culture building which we have distilled as follows:

Meet your teams where they are and where they are going: use objective-centered risk assessment, which focuses on the opportunities that are your business partners' goals, the activities required to meet those goals, and the vulnerabilities arising from those activities.

Find inclusive ways to get input on the practical realities on the ground: Regularly collect input about goals, activities, and vulnerabilities to learn about any changes or real-time updates. Use humility and curiosity in gathering risk intelligence, and don't rely only on the inputs or guesswork of senior team leaders or corporate service professionals like compliance officers or lawyers.

Scale and automate the regular collection and analysis of this information: leverage crowdsourcing methods and various integrated listening channels to allow stakeholders to easily share information. Encourage this sharing of information by demonstrating that you are listening and showing how it has led to you making better-informed decisions. Celebrate the best ideas and the impact they are having.

Make risk intelligence available to provide relevant information and answers fast. Real-time data is most beneficial to team members navigating their own unique journeys. Motivate crowd sharing, make it easy, and use prompts to encourage enduring sharing behaviors.

Leverage your culture-building community: Other culture builders across your industry or region are an excellent source of intelligence and insights. Find ways to collaborate to share industry best practices and learn from each other as a form of crowdsourcing.

In her book, *Living Your Best Compliance Life: 65 Hacks and Cheat Codes to Level Up Your Ethics and Compliance Program*, Mary Shirley explains how much of her inspiration has come from the fantastic compliance community she has built around her. With the support of Corporate Compliance Insights and the Compliance Podcast Network, Mary and

Lisa Fine created the *Great Women in Compliance Podcast* community, which has become a hot spot for crowdsourcing and peer ideation. Hemma is now a co-host of that podcast, available CorporateComplianceInsights.com, and her guests are often a source of inspiration and ideas for her work.

Here's a Bright Idea

In design thinking, the key concept to master is the user experience (UX). According to Carsten Tams, a compliance consultant known as the Ethical Business Architect, "Design thinking offers a well-structured process and a practical, easy-to-use toolbox of methods that [...] practitioners can use to find innovative and human-centered solutions for increasing program engagement. The stages of the design process consist of understanding users and defining the design challenge, ideating and prioritizing ideas for solutions, and prototyping and testing the most promising ideas."

Using the concept of design sprints, you could design virtual workshops that allow you to collect relevant information from large groups of employees in an accelerated way, using Miro or Jam boards.

For example, as part of a larger project to dig deep into third-party risk management, consider conducting initial preparation sessions with small focus groups or in 1:1 meetings to canvass information about the Partner-facing team's main goals and objectives and the specific activities they typically carry out to meet those objectives. A simple way to do this is to collect information on the entire life cycle of an interaction with a Partner or other types of third-party.

Then, when assessing that list of activities or life-cycle, set up sessions to crowdsource (from a range of employees) the types of vulnerabilities from business activities, organizational factors, and cultural factors to which your partner team might be exposed as a result of those activities. This includes facilitating discussions to elicit information from the employees on the ground as to how this vulnerability is likely to show up in practice and how this might vary by region.

Once you have collected this information, you could crowdsource ideas on the best practical approaches to handling those risks and the conditions your organization would need to create to achieve outcomes at scale. In this way, the employees can start coaching *you* on relevant risk management for culture building.

You can then collate and analyze the information you have obtained and use it to define your communication strategies and training priorities. This allows you to consider intentionally how to ensure that information is available to relevant persons throughout the life cycle of third-party interactions and engagements.

Experimenting with different ways to encourage crowdsourcing

We know that humans don't naturally like to talk about what could possibly go wrong on their watch, perhaps because we have a certain cognitive dissonance or hubris about our control over our experiences or just because it feels uncomfortable and even counterproductive to confront the worst-case scenarios. Culture builders are well versed in leveraging case studies, whether hypothetical or based on real-life events, to spark relevant discussion and thinking without putting the teams they serve on the defensive.

Near-miss reporting

Near-miss reporting is another excellent way to crowdsource risk information and identify red flags or hotspots. Used widely in the aviation industry, by surgeons, and in workplace safety, the idea is that near misses must be reported to obtain useful information about vulnerabilities and how to avoid them.

For example, employees traveling for work through an airport notorious for customs officers requesting bribes could share their stories of how they said no and share guidance with others based on their experience of what works to avoid such situations. This includes advice like not wearing branded clothing or carrying items that advertise that you work for a global company, not carrying cash, declining clearly and loudly when necessary, requesting official invoices or receipts to prove the legitimacy of fees, and asking for and using the officer's name and badge number. While not foolproof, these simple activities can put off an unscrupulous agent from persisting with their request. With this knowledge, a company might be able to decide to provide support for those employees not to have to travel through the specific airport where possible, and even report such behavior to local authorities.

Practice saying no thank you

In another example, employees might express concern, embarrassment, or even fear of causing offense when they are required to decline excessive gifts or meals from business partners. Consider the development of a workshop called "The Art of Saying No Thank You" - where participants can share stories of what works and what doesn't, and others can practice explaining the benefits of that policy in their own words, rather than just saying - "because my compliance team says it is unethical."

Consider having staff work in pairs to practice the "Three Whys" game, where the person acting as the gift giver would ask "but why?" three times, forcing the person being offered the gift to articulate the actual reason for having to say no underlying the "policy."

In one practice example, an employee declined by saying they weren't available to attend a premier sports event with a partner on a specific date. The partner said, "No problem - we have season tickets - how about the week after next?" There was no escaping the offer. Rather than pretend she was unavailable indefinitely, the employee knew she had to offer a more sincere explanation and politely decline the offer with an explanation. She could state that she didn't want her acceptance of expensive tickets to the event to give the appearance of a *quid pro quo*, especially as they were in current talks about a competitive bid. They could both agree that they didn't want anything to jeopardize that process.

Another practical example of crowdsourcing information at scale

Using a Jamboard or Miroboard to ask questions can be a great way to elicit ideation on risk management from your teams on the ground, allowing speedy and simultaneous information gathering at scale, including the option for doing so anonymously. It is easy to set up a board, ask questions, and allow your participants to add real-time comments. Whether you use virtual sticky notes, emoticons, comments, or other creative inputs to suit your style, this method allows you to get answers fast, even from the proverbial quiet ones in the "back of the room."

You might also use a virtual collaboration board to do a perceptions assessment. The inspiration for this idea came from an exercise a political candidate used to produce campaign talking points based on his position relative to his opponent.

In the example below entitled *Bridging the Gap*, a very brave compliance team wanted to allow its business partners a space to talk about their perceptions of the ethics and compliance team and themselves relative to each other. In a safe space, where honest feedback was requested, and while there was plenty of positive feedback, some business partners shared honestly that they saw the compliance team as 'the police,' or 'out of touch with reality,' or too 'risk averse' and 'too wordy in communications.' Ouch - but what a gift to listen with curiosity and adapt. The immediate result for culture-builders was trust-building, clearing out some of the elephants in the room and allowing participants to feel seen, heard, and valued. You will find that an exercise like this produces some very relevant perspectives and actionable insights, which, you could use in turn to initiate a "Stop, Start, Continue" board to discuss with your culture-building team.

BRIGHT IDEAS FOR CROWDSOURCING INTELLIGENCE

```
                    BRIDGING THE GAP EXERCISE

  How the Business Teams view Compliance?   How Compliance views the Business Teams?




  How Compliance views itself?              How the Business Teams view themselves?




  6 mins      Instructions:            THANK
                • Use the stickies to add your thoughts.   YOU      2 mins
                • Organize similar ideas or clusters on the board
                • Use the dots to agree or prioritize
```

Bridging the Gap is an exercise conducted on a virtual collaboration board created in Miro. Participants can simultaneously and anonymously add their thoughts to the board using virtual Post-its and dots.

Using non-confrontational discussion methods

Reviewing the latest enforcement actions involving competitors who share your goals and business objectives and are seeking the same opportunities as your organization is an excellent way to accelerate identifying the risks to which your teams might be exposed. This is a form of non-confrontational discussion.

For example, your team could use a virtual collaboration board to review an enforcement case involving a key risk area for your organization. You might consider a scenario where a competitor was alleged to have been involved with third parties paying bribes to government officials. Lean in here with humility and curiosity - how could this happen over there? Here are some powerful, curious coaching questions you can ask to get to the risk intelligence:

- Could this happen here?
- What conditions allowed it to happen there?
- How do we avoid this here?
- What systems could we change or improve to avoid this in the future?
- What communications (and with whom) would be helpful to achieve this?

There's something magical about the non-confrontational discussion stemming from a real-life story that isn't yours (yet) but is contextually relevant. The teams that deal with external partners daily can offer a relevant perspective on the likelihood of certain third-party risks based on the industry, culture, and current conditions (including knowledge, awareness, and competing pressures.) Often, they have good ideas on how to monitor those risks and great practical ideas on how to mitigate those risks in a reasonable and feasible way.

The reverse brainstorm

Another powerful tool is the 'reverse brainstorm', where you identify the goal or define success, notice the opposite of the goal or define failure, and then brainstorm the conditions and activities that are most likely to bring about that failure. Powerful coaching questions for a reverse brainstorm on a competitor's misfortune could be:

- If we wanted to bring about these negative behaviors or outcomes, what conditions would we need to create here? Be creative. For example, if we wanted to dissuade speaking up at our company, what would we need to do?
- Are we creating (even inadvertently) any of those conditions here? Sometimes, despite our best intentions, we find that we might have

some blind spots and potential gaps we can address.

As a bonus, these collaborative sessions can also achieve a lot for the culture you are trying to create - they are trust-building (inclusion, empathy), risk assessment (curious, humble), and training (informative, interactive, collaborative) all in one.

The application in your pocket?

But what about scaling this method and having a crowdsourcing application at your fingertips for culture building? Can we start thinking about culture and compliance as a service? Imagine a bot in your software that helps you get answers to the most pressing questions to and from your team members, and fast: a digital front door that serves as a portal for sharing information, processing relevant intakes such as reporting and approvals, and creating a culture of crowdsourcing.

This can be done with a live agent or an agentless bot programmed with frequently asked questions and prompts or requests for feedback. You might leverage generative AI to read your policies and generate answers to the specific questions of your team members. Customer relationship management tools have long been leveraged in this way: taking in product or service feedback, getting answers to customers quickly, and equipping live or virtual agents with ways to mine data for this purpose. Machine learning and large language models can also be used to synthesize data and detect trends.

Inspired by the applications that help drivers on road trips into Washington, D.C. and beyond? If so, think about how you might replicate that ease and customer experience for your culture and watch this space.

Our Challenge to You

Ask yourself:

- What applications do you use that are examples of *culture building in the wild*?
- Are there any ideas that you can bring back to your function?
- What are the inputs for your risk assessments?
- In what ways can you upgrade those inputs to incorporate more regular inputs and real-time information?
- Are you assessing risk relevant to the company's goals, desired objectives, and key results?
- Is there a way to get relevant answers to your team members faster?
- How can you leverage and lean in on a community of culture builders to share ideas and innovate?

Consider:

- Reviewing your objectives as a culture-building function to ensure they are designed around the vulnerabilities associated with your company's goals and activities.
- Crowdsourcing as a means of enhancing your risk intelligence, at least for your highest-risk areas.
- Leveraging technology to get answers to your employees fast or to crowdsource real-time data and information from them.
- Joining or creating a benchmarking group to crowdsource industry

best practices and lessons learned.

Parting Thoughts on Crowdsourcing Risk Intelligence

> "You don't own your brand anymore. Honor the crowd's co-ownership of your brand."
> – Shelley Kuipers

The call to "honor the crowd" is a beautiful way to summarize this chapter. Your culture is your brand, and it is co-owned by the members of the organization or group. Even when a healthy tone at the top is set for the culture, the various members will create and experience the culture every day. If left unmanaged, it might become a moving target. It stands to reason that we should embrace this phenomenon and lean into regularly crowdsourcing intelligence about that culture from the members. Humans are social creatures, and we will adapt and change based on the conditions in which we find ourselves. The best insight into those conditions will come from creatively engaging the humans that make up your culture to obtain concrete information about what works and what doesn't, as well as ideas and inspiration for solutions.

8

A Guide to Peer Ideation

A Guide to Peer Ideation

A key theme throughout the examples we have shared in this book is a human-centered approach to ideation for culture-building that leverages the strengths and insights of various stakeholders, including, most importantly, the humans we serve as members of that culture. These are the individuals and teams we ask to create and own the culture and to manage various risks, operationalize controls, make ethical decisions, and implement our guidance.

There are many ways to get to this information, such as interviews and prompts for feedback. You might ask group members to share stories, fill out surveys or questionnaires, and participate in focus groups or discussion circles.

One powerful and highly effective method for eliciting input is the peer coaching model. This model provides an opportunity to create and cultivate supportive relationships within an organization by leveraging the insights and ideas of other group or peer coaching members.

With this method, a group or circle can come together with the specific goal of collectively ideating to solve problems and achieve goals. The group might agree on some ground rules like those in the image below. The group or circle should be set up to consist of 'peers' in the broadest sense, with or without prior knowledge or expertise in the subject matter, and representing all levels of seniority. In fact, such diversity of representation in the group can produce compelling insights, especially if group members don't know each other's roles and titles.

The Concept: Ideation Circles Using The Peer Coaching Method

Form a circle of peers, ideally with five to six members. This model works well for groups as small as three and as many as 12, depending on the time you can allocate to the exercise. You can also use it with large groups broken into break-out circles. Importantly, circle members do not have to be "peers" in the literal sense nor experts in the field of inquiry. Some of the most potent peer coaching comes from fellow coaches who do not work in your field or industry and are not constrained by your experience. You might even avoid doing introductions in a newly formed group at the beginning of the session to ensure that inputs aren't received differently depending on profession, title, or leveling.

The group can operate in person or virtually. Share any ground rules that work best for the group to set the tone and intention. You can use something simple, like the three C's in the sample infographic below, calling for confidentiality, communication, and commitment.

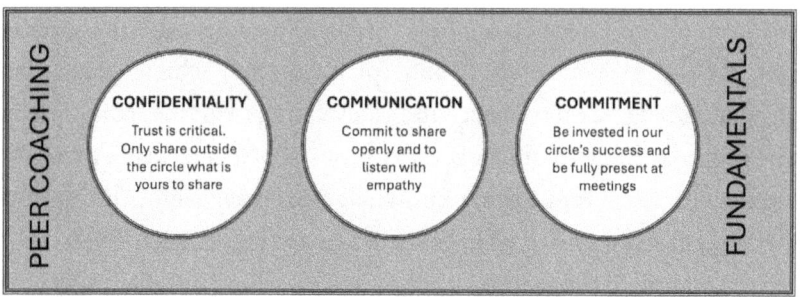

Sample infographic with peer coaching fundamentals created in Microsoft PowerPoint

Peer coaching is a very simple repeatable model. To kick off the peer coaching, one member of a group (the "coachee") will pose a question or problem statement to the group of their peers (the "coaches"). Then, the coachee will respond to any clarifying questions from the coaches about what the coachee is trying to achieve. Next, the coachee will listen quietly as the peer coaches ideate on that problem statement through curious coaching questions. Finally, the coachee will collect their thoughts through either quiet reflection or sharing with the coaches.

The fundamental rule here is that the peer coaches are not to give *advice*. The goal is to ideate through curiosity and provide food for thought, leaving the coachee with agency in the ultimate decision-making process.

Peer coaches are limited to asking curious coaching questions about the problem statement - only questions - and not providing answers.

In this format, their contributions will be thought-provoking - without requiring the coachee to respond or react in the moment. Even if you are tempted to formulate a question that appears to have an idea or give some advice, that is much better than directly making suggestions. Framing your thoughts as questions allows you to present them with curiosity. This small effort can deflect any natural psychological defenses on the part of the coachee.

Here is an example. Can you hear the difference?

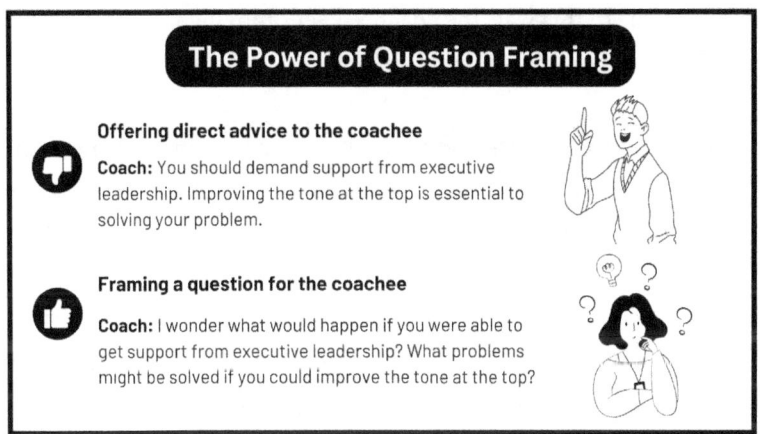

An infographic made in Canva with images and text showing a comparison between giving advice and asking a curious coaching question.

Coaches might ask curious questions about potential pathways to the goal, perceived obstacles, mindset adjustments, blind spots, operational tips and tricks, or leadership devices. These questions can disrupt any potential bias or habitual behaviors that too often derail the best-laid plans. All of this is done in a psychologically safe and supportive manner, acknowledging multiple pathways to success without judgment, ego, pressure, or conditions.

After a defined period of coaching, the final step is to allow the coachee some brief reflection time at the end of the coaching portion. Having been figuratively (or perhaps literally) on mute during the coaching portion - the coachee is now permitted to speak again. The coachee might thank the coaches for their input without more, share or quietly consider the impact of these different perspectives on their thinking, and choose to leverage those perspectives to make informed decisions as they see fit. In this way, the coachee keeps moving towards *their* next right thing with ownership and agency.

The circle can then rotate and reorganize to allow another member to take the role of the coachee and to have others serve in the role of a peer coach, whether in the same session or at a subsequent meeting.

Through a structured and repeatable process of Consulting, Clarifying, Coaching, and Collection, the 4 Cs peer coaching model prompts unencumbered thinking by the group and unlocks rich insights. The coachees can benefit from multiple perspectives and the ideation presented through questions. They are then given space to listen and then move forward to confidently determine what courses of action might work best for their circumstances while deftly navigating potential blind spots. This process often shines a light on a new way of approaching the issue and allows the coachee to escape the limitations that may have been preventing them from finding their best solution pathways alone or in silo.

A GUIDE TO PEER IDEATION

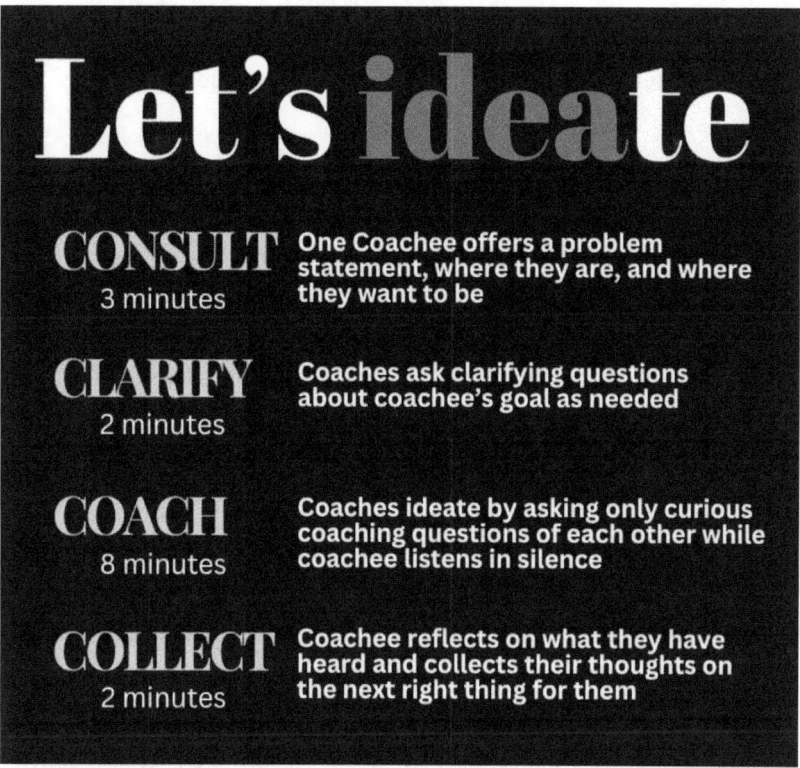

A flyer created in Canva for an Ideation session run by the authors at the Society of Corporate Compliance and Ethics's 23rd Annual Compliance and Ethics Institute in Grapevine, Texas - showing the 4 C's of Peer Coaching with sample timings for each part and a short description of each.

Here's a sample Peer Ideation session:

Part 1 - CONSULT:

Say you're looking for ways to ensure employees feel safe speaking up in your organization. As a coachee - you would first define your problem statement. You might describe to your coaches:

1. your goal
2. where you are today
3. where you would like to be
4. the primary challenges you face or obstacles you foresee

You would then request a peer coaching consultation. Here's an example:

(Coachee)
I am looking for ways to improve the speak-up culture at my organization.

Today we have a hotline tool that we launched a year ago and communicated to all employees. It is also referenced in the Code of Conduct and annual compliance training. We have had very few reports in our first year. We recently ran an ethical culture survey, and the results weren't great. Many of our employees said they were unlikely to report for fear of retaliation.

I would like to improve this for my organization

I would appreciate some peer ideation on this.

Part 2 - CLARIFY:

After the coachee has set out the problem statement, the peer coaches are given a few minutes to ask any clarifying questions that will help them understand the coachee's dilemma and goals.

Here are a couple of examples for our scenario:

(Coach 1)
Have I understood correctly that you want to see the number of hotline reports increase?

(Coachee)
Yes, and I'd like see what we can do about the perceived threat of retaliation.

(Coach 2)
What percentage of those surveyed said they were unlikely to report for fear of retaliation?

(Coachee)
65%

Part 3 - COACH:

Next, the peer coaches begin to ideate on the problem statement presented. The most important rule for this part is that the coaches are only permitted to ask curious coaching questions. They must refrain from making recommendations or giving advice, however tempting that may be.

During this time, the coachee should refrain from responding or interrupting. Coachees can instead listen intently and take notes as needed. Coaches may find it hard not to fix things or give advice, but they must refrain. A monitor or guide can be appointed to monitor this rule in action and kindly nudge any fixers back to coaching questions. Below are examples of what peer coaching might sound like.

Sample questions that the peer coaches might ask of each other include:

- *I would be curious about what is behind those survey results.*
- *I wonder what might be causing those low numbers.*
- *Are there follow-up questions to survey participants or a focus group that might provide more context to the results?*
- *What does her team need to do to feel good about the results?*
- *I wonder if the issue underlying the survey results is fear of retaliation, or futility, or some other bad experience with speaking up?*
- *What else might be true in this organization?*
- *Could there be ways in which leadership is inadvertently dissuading reporting that could be examined and addressed?*
- *What if the reticence is because of the behaviors of management?*
- *What strategies might help them address that?*
- *Is there regulatory guidance on how to improve a whistleblower culture that she could leverage?*
- *Is there a historical practice at this organization that has become an urban legend or myth that could be addressed by current leadership?*
- *Are there any good examples of investigation outcomes and lessons learned that can be shared with the employees?*
- *What is the immediate goal of this team?*
- *What might be the most straightforward, most accessible initiatives that will have an immediate impact?*
- *Would it be different if her team focused on X instead of Y?*
- *Is their track record enforcing the non-retaliation policy relevant?*
- *Is there any particular training could address this issue directly? How?*
- *How many reports would be enough?*
- *What other options does the team have for listening channels?*
- *What opportunities are there to remind participants during investigations about the retaliation policy?*
- *What is the change they are seeking?*
- *What does success look like?*
- *What is the motivation for wanting more reports at this time?*

- *Do the survey results show that the issue is concentrated in a particular team or region?*
- *What regional or cultural issues may be in play?*
- *I wonder if there is a disconnect in expectations for different levels of employees?*
- *What fear or insecurity might be holding the team back?*
- *What benchmarking might be available in her industry on how to improve those culture survey results?*
- *Could they improve the user experience in the hotline tool?*
- *What type of speak up or listen up campaign might work for their employees?*
- *I wonder if there is an opportunity to communicate more about the relatively new hotline tool?*

Part 4 - COLLECT:

The ideation session is then followed by a short reflection on the part of the coachee to allow her to collect her thoughts. She might use this time to share the impacts of the coaching session, including highlights, new ideas, or key takeaways. She may also use the time to sit in quiet reflection, speaking only to thank the peer coaches for their time.

This could look something like the following:

(Coachee).
    Thank you for your questions and thoughtful ideas. This has been immensely helpful, and I have written down some great takeaways. I already feel like I have some ideas for concrete action as we move towards the next right thing for our organization.

These peer coaching groups or circles are easy to set up, self-sustaining, inexpensive to operate, and flexible enough to apply to various circumstances. While a facilitator can be helpful, assigning the role of timekeeper and monitor to one group member is easy. Each circle member can take turns sharing a problem statement to benefit from the process. Peer coaching circles are intended to provide the psychological safety necessary to build trust, unlock insights, and dig a little deeper into the why, why not, what, and how - towards reaching our goals.

Our Challenge to You

Ask yourself:

- Are you tired of trying the same thing and hoping for different results? Could you inject some fresh ideas with peer ideation?
- Are there goals where you feel a little stuck? Could you benefit from some curious coaching questions about why?
- Is there a team whose buy-in you need on a project? Could you ask them to participate in peer coaching to look for pathways to getting that project done?
- Is your team working in silos on different projects? Could you use peer coaching to increase connection and collaboration?

Consider:

- Seeking ideas the next time you refresh your code of conduct or policies using a peer coaching session.

- Using peer coaching sessions as break-out sessions at your next training event.
- Conducting a pre-mortem or a table top exercise, using the peer coaching model.
- Using peer coaching to solve hypothetical problems as a learning and engagement tool.
- Trying a peer coaching model with your family, friends, or a group of children. This could be about a work or personal challenge, or just about planning an upcoming trip or a meal. Participants might surprise you with their insights and perspectives. Inspiration is everywhere.
- Using a peer coaching circle to get help on behavior design. Ask peers for help for ideas on the specific behaviors you might want in the culture you are building. Collect those ideas and then prioritize facilitating the most feasible and impactful. Check out the work of Stanford Behavior Design expert Dr. BJ Fogg for more inspiration here, in particular the Fogg Behavior Design Model and his "Magic Wand," "Swarm of Behaviors," and "Focus Mapping" methods.

Parting Thoughts on Peer Ideation

> "There are three main reasons Circles work. As humans we enjoy being with others, we are more creative in groups, and we are more courageous when with others."
> – Maureen F. Fitzgerald, PhD

Ideation takes courage by its very nature and requires us to step away from the comfort of existing methods and consider the as-yet-unknown or untried. It is fueled by inspiration and imagination, and the potential rewards are amplified exponentially when we practice it in groups. It is daring to grow and iterate on existing methods. Peer coaching leverages the power of collaboration and collective ideation, where you can open up a challenge to insights from your peers. Culture building is inherently a team sport - the players, the opposing team, the spectators, the fans, the vendors and volunteers, and even those outside the stadium will all have valuable vantage points.

Peer coaching allows for combinatorial innovation and bright aha moments. It is designed to mitigate the vulnerability and discomfort of asking for advice and then perhaps choosing to go another way. It allows for agency and ownership in the creative process while accelerating the collection of diverse perspectives.

It is generous and mutual and a great leveler in terms of potential sources of inspiration. It is a skill that can be honed and leveraged to give and receive support. Through peer coaching, you can welcome unconditional ideation, drawing on the wisdom and perspective of supportive bystanders while retaining agency to own your decisions on the next right thing. Start a 4Cs peer ideation circle today and create some magic!

Conclusion

"Culture is not an initiative. Culture is the enabler of all initiatives."
– Larry Senn

This book is for culture builders who, through their ideas and actions, inspire others to improve the conditions in which people work, live, and play. Your work is important, and it is your energy and perseverance that will motivate the values-driven behaviors that bring about collective ease and peace of mind.

The beauty of culture-building is that it is inherently a shared responsibility. Healthy and productive cultures are a common goal, and many of us have valuable perspectives and experiences of what works and what doesn't.

Together, we can do the challenging and rewarding work of creating conditions where people thrive. Ideation is a natural and accessible tool to have in your tool belt when building culture, and peer coaching is a reliable way to leverage the insights of the various members of your culture. Inspiration is everywhere, and we hope you will enjoy practicing the art of ideation for culture building and beyond.

Join the Community

We welcome you to join the community of ideators. Use the QR Code below to access our LinkedIn group. There, you will find bonus content and be able to share your ideas for ideation with other culture builders.

Hemma Ramrattan Lomax, Ph.D
The Compliance Coach
Award Winning Corporate Ethics
and Compliance Executive
Founder of COMPAAS 360 and
The Compliance Coaches Institute

Ashley Dubriwny, M.Ed, CCEP-I
Culture Strategist
HR & Ethics Leader - Speaker
Writer - Trust Builder
Champion of people,
integrity, and possibility.

JOIN THE COMMUNITY
Ideation Station
LinkedIn Group.
Come for the ideas,
stay for the community.

Flyer produced in Canva showing AI-generated images of the authors and a QR Code you can use to access and join our Ideation Station LinkedIn community.

If you enjoyed reading this book, please consider sharing your thoughts in a review on Amazon.com or Goodreads.com. We'd love to hear from you.

Also by Hemma Lomax & Ashley Dubriwny

The Art of Ideation
Ideas can help spark initiatives, but we think culture builders deserve more than just ideas. By understanding the concepts of ideating, you can develop the skill of generating your own bright ideas and optimize your idea-generating success with peer ideation techniques.

The Art of Implementation
Implementation is where culture comes alive — where vision meets action, where ideas find form, and where organizations build trust that lasts.

The Art of Celebration
The Art of Celebration shows leaders and culture builders how acknowledgment shapes the future. With insights from neuroscience, appreciative inquiry, and creative rituals, it reveals how intentional celebration fuels resilience, belonging, and joy.

www.ingramcontent.com/pod-product-compliance
Lightning Source LLC
Chambersburg PA
CBHW070143230526
45471CB00002B/497